The Classic
Layout Designs
of John Armstrong

A compilation
of ideas and
commentary
from the dean
of custom
layout designers

KALMBACH
BOOKS

Printed in the United States of America

01 02 03 04 05 06 07 08 09   10 9 8 7 6 5 4 3 2 1

Visit our website at
http://kalmbachbooks.com
Secure online ordering available

Publisher's Cataloging-in-Publication
(Provided by Quality Books, Inc.

Armstrong, John H.
    The classic layout / designs of John Armstrong. —
  1st ed.
    p. cm.
    ISBN 0-89024-417-0

    1. Railroads—Models. 2. Railroads—Track.
I. Title.

TF197.A76 2001   625.1'9
                            QBI00-902094

Art director: Kristi Ludwig
Book design: Sabine Beaupré

The material in this book has previously appeared as articles in *Model Railroader*
magazine and various Kalmbach books. They are reprinted in their entirety and
include an occasional reference to an item elsewhere in the same issue or in a
previous issue.

Contents

Harper's Ferry Vignette

This layout, patterned after a small portion of a

real railroad, features simple operation and excellent

modeling possibilities in a minimum of space

L ET'S SUPPOSE you like big motive power and mainline trains—in fact, that you have already built an eight-car abbreviation of the Capitol Limited with three F-3 units to haul it. As a thoroughgoing Baltimore & Ohio fan, you have remodeled a kit Pacific into a big blue President and scratchbuilt a "Big Six" 2-10-2. You have already built enough freight equipment to load down the articulated you are seriously considering as the next motive-power-construction project. But you look at the space situation and are forced to the conclusion that, if you use suitable curve radii for the big locomotives, a Christmas tree oval is just about all there's room for. What can you do?

Well, you can build glass cases and put the models in them. You can switch to branchline or old-time stuff—but that's strictly a second-choice proposition. You can sell the equipment, go into a smaller gauge, and give up a lot of the

detail, heft, and realism of the bigger gauge you started in.

But let's think it over. Since you chose to put your time into the construction of fine rolling stock, you're probably not primarily interested in timetable or complicated point-to-point operation. Perhaps a layout would be well worthwhile if it could provide a single scene, detailed as painstakingly as your models, in which your *Capitol Limited* could be shown off in reasonably lifelike operation.

For ideas on how to accomplish this, we can study the theater, where there have been a few hundred years of experience in showing a realistic portion of life in a small space. First, all the action is made to take place in a compact but completely enclosed area—the stage itself. Only the characters that have a part in the action of the moment are visible. Other parts of the theater are darkened, and the passageways, ladders, and other gear necessary to get the actor to his

entrance on cue are hidden from view.

The application to our problem is obvious—we can use loops, cutoffs, and sneakoffs as required, but they must be "backstage." This means that most of what little track we have will be hidden,

Author's Insight

For two years or so from the 1952 start of the "Track Plan of the Month" series in *Model Railroader* I actually did turn out articles at almost that rate. So, I was grateful that editor John Page wanted small layouts such as HO 4 x 8s. Most could handle only short trains. A bigger-time scenario in such a space could call for a worthy mainline consist to emerge from hiding, traverse as long a course as possible within the layout's confines—a diagonal—and disappear. Is there some piece of railroad with trackage and terrain so concentrated that we can model a panorama of almost full-scale proportions?

At Harper's Ferry the Baltimore & Ohio provides just that.

Along its double-track main line (in any track plan of 10 to 15 squares of any dimension, double track makes for far more operating variety than single) in less than a half mile there are a tunnel, quarry-branch junction, long bridge, station, hillside town, and steep-sided cut. Too bad there are only a few other such compact, rugged locales elsewhere for us to model—Storm King (New York) comes to mind.

With the aid of steep (but out-of-sight) grades and track secluded by a curved backdrop, this 6 x 10 layout also manages to accommodate 30 or 40 car-lengths of staging trackage. Mainline tastes in a shortline space? Look for a vignette!

BALTIMORE & OHIO RR.

but the realism of the action on the part remaining will be increased more than enough to compensate. Hiding the unrealistic part of the trackage, though, means that several tunnels, cliffs, and sharp curves may be necessary, and several of these "stagey" props in a small space aren't likely to look genuine.

Maybe we can get around this trouble by "inverse rationalization," or the Fibber McGee [An old-time radio comedian. —Ed.] approach. Fibber attacked the problem of developing a supersonic airplane by a novel and previously overlooked method—he decided to try to make a slower sound instead of a faster plane. So, we can look for a place on the real railroad that looks like a diorama. This we can then copy in detail, the actual dimensions perhaps fore-

shortened somewhat, but the general scene made authentic by the existence of a prototype.

If we try this scheme on the B&O, the place we're likely to think of first is Harper's Ferry. Here we have steep bluffs, a short tunnel, a village clinging to a side hill, a rock-strewn river, and a variety of bridges. Harper's Ferry itself has several features strongly reminiscent of model attempts to get everything conceivable into a given space. There's an underpass which (because of new bridge construction and road rerouting) doesn't go anywhere in particular; a station platform extending out over the river; an old tooth powder ad painted on a cliff above the tracks; and, right between the main line and a siding, a formal sunken garden! In short,

This photo of Harper's Ferry, West Virginia, shows the area featured in the track plan. B&O branch-line and a highway share truss bridge at left. Watchmen at each end stop autos when trains approach.

the scene simply reeks with the kind of detail that's easy to model.

The accompanying track plan shows how the basic layout at Harper's Ferry can help us create a realistic mainline scene in a total space three by five times the minimum track radius, with a little branchline operation thrown in for good measure. What we see as we look at the layout from the west side is a stretch of the B&O's double-track main line. It comes out of a short tunnel on the Maryland side of the Potomac, crosses a multi-span deck girder bridge,

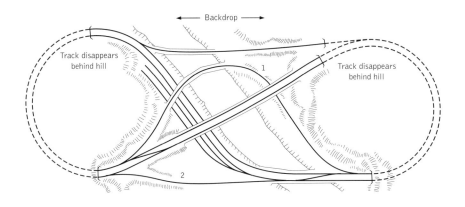

Here is an alternative arrangement of the same basic track plan that conceals only the ends of the loops. Cutoffs 1 and 2 both permit reversing moves so that either may be eliminated if desired. Both, however, are plausible as interchange tracks between two double-track lines.

and disappears beneath our vantage point on the West Virginia side. Harper's Ferry station, complete with pedestrian subway under the busy tracks, is on the curve at the river's edge. The Shenandoah Valley branch to Winchester and Strasburg Junction, Virginia, switches from the main at the very mouth of the tunnel and crosses on a separate bridge. Behind this second bridge the Shenandoah River joins the Potomac from the south. Beyond it lies a corner of Virginia, connected to Maryland by a high-level bridge leading to a road that clings to another steep mountainside. Along the Maryland bank of the Potomac are the remains of the old Chesapeake & Ohio canal.

A sharply curved siding off the branch line in front of the Harper's Ferry siding looks as if it might formerly have been the main line before the curvature was reduced by building the present bridge; as a matter of fact, it was. The siding is always ready for emergency reconnection to serve as the main line again if the bridge should be blocked for some reason or other (as it was briefly in 1951, by fire). Still another row of piers, now decaying into little tree-covered rock piles, marks the location of an earlier B&O bridge across the Potomac, which later ended its days carrying a road.

Underneath this tranquil scene lies the most "tinplatish" of layouts—a double-track figure eight with two reversing connections along the sides. This basic plan, unrealistic as it would be if left completely exposed, suits our purpose well. Two trains can run continuously on the main line without interference. Either can reverse its direction of travel via the appropriate cutoff, and the cutoff on the south side is long enough to hold two short trains so that up to four trains

can be handled if need be. The operation in this case appears to be quite logical—various trains running back and forth on the main line, in no particular sequence and with no tendency for operation to favor one direction of travel or the other. Just how this is accomplished, however, is well concealed, as it should be.

A layout as simple as this won't take long to get into operation, although you'll probably spend plenty of time on the scenery in bringing it up to the standards of your rolling stock. Sooner or later, then, you'll be back at the bench turning out more rolling stock. So, a place has been provided where several more trains can be stored ready to enter the main line any time. Our subterranean "Brunswick Yards" are an insult to the B&O's enormous classification layout, which stretches for more than eight miles between the two main tracks through Brunswick, Md. (5 miles east of Harper's Ferry), but using the name is handy.

DIMENSIONS

	HO	S	O
Scale of drawing	¾"	½"	⅜"
Size of squares	24"	36"	48"
Length overall	10'-0"	15'-0"	20'-0"
Width overall	6'-0"	9'-0"	12'-0"
Minimum radius			
Main line	24"	36"	48"
Branch line	18"	27"	36"
Multiply track elevation figures by	1	1½	2
Turnouts	Main line and Brunswick are No. 6; branch, No. 4.		

Gaps necessary only for automatic speed regulation not shown.

The underground storage tracks make it possible to leave much of your equipment made up in trains and ready to run without handling, while at the same time collecting little dust. You might add that it's morally better to be able to bring it forth with a locomotive, too. There is enough of a lead clear of the main line coming out of Brunswick to allow for changes of train consist without either stopping the passing parade or getting ulcers.

We need some mild interference with mainline traffic to spice up the operation, though, and a little branchline business never hurts any layout. We can get both by including a train movement that accounts for much of the traffic on the Shenandoah Valley branch. Millville, West Virginia, four miles down the branch from junction A, has extensive quarries that call for two or three trains a day to bring in empties and haul out loads of crushed rock. We use modeler's license and move Millville right up behind Harper's Ferry. Then, by taking advantage of the fact that a quarry can have vertical walls, we can have quite reasonable scenic separation between main line and branch without running out of space.

Two or three times a day a crew will leave Brunswick with the quarry empties, trade them at Millville for the loads of rock, and do any switching needed at Harper's Ferry. To preserve the appearance of correct operation, of course, this train should approach Harper's Ferry from the east and return in the same way. This maneuver can be handled in two ways. If no crossover connection between the two mainline tracks is provided at junction A, it will be necessary to operate starting clockwise over the South Cutoff and then on the lefthand track from the end of the cutoff track to the junction when going from Brunswick to Millville. This may block the main a bit more than you desire.

The alternative is to locate a crossover near junction A, as shown in the plan. This crossover completes a "reversing loop" in the electrical sense, so the proper reversible leads must be provided to one of the mainline blocks in which the crossover occurs. It's interesting to note that without this connection between the two main tracks there is no reversing loop, even though the same train can pass Harper's Ferry in either direction. The fact that the normal direction of travel on any one track is always the same accounts for this.

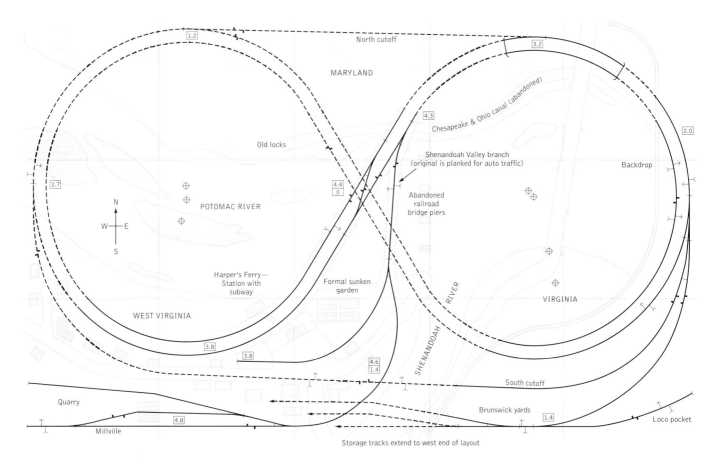

Now we should come to grips with a few practical problems in the construction of a layout like this. The B&O, despite the ruggedness of the terrain at Harper's Ferry, is running on a typical "water grade," and we should have no visible track on a noticeable incline. The bridge should be a fair distance above the water. Even then, there is very little clearance for a bridge plus piers. A way to get around this is to provide a rapids running diagonally under the bridges and the river modeled at high-water stage to make the short piers look realistic. With our invisible tracks below the river, we will need about 3.3 percent grades on the main loop and almost 4 percent on the rear cutoff track. The latter track is always operated in the downhill direction, so it's no problem. The main-line grades, fortunately, are somewhat self-compensating in that the rear end of any fairly long train will still be going downhill at the time the locomotive is laboring up the worst part of the grade.

As we noted earlier, this layout is designed to accommodate mainline equipment and make it look at home, so if you have or want an articulated, it will fit right into the picture. When the B&O was in its heyday, most freight through Harper's Ferry was pulled by big EM-1 2-8-8-4s, with 2-10-2s and Mikes doing

their part too. Don't overlook the operating interest of having passenger trains stop at the station—11 of the 22 daily trains stopped, including the lengthy Baltimore-Detroit *Ambassador*.

The branch is laid out with no. 4 turnouts, so you are restricted to branchline motive power—certainly nothing bigger than a 2-8-2. If, like so many thousand others, you have a Dockside or other small switcher, it will be comfortably at home in the quarry.

Chances are, though, that you yourself aren't a B&O modeler, and that there are a good many other places that interest you more than Harper's Ferry. The basic layout plan, with or without the branch line, is surprisingly adaptable to other places and other railroads. If you want a river-crossing scene for a freelance line, simply reverse Harper's Ferry from right to left, and no one will recognize it. If you do this, it will take a little tinkering with the storage area to fit it in with right-hand double-track operation, unless you take the easy way out and say that your road runs left-handed like the C&NW.

The second plan shown is basically identical in track scheme, but here the lines have been twisted to represent a crossing of two double-track lines of the same railroad. Connecting tracks link the

two main lines; to get a workable grade, all the tracks are sharply curved and interlaced, and four bridges across the river are needed. The scene is quite typical of actual junctions in the heavy-traffic territory of Pennsylvania and eastern Ohio, where even short branches may be double track and a railroad either follows a river valley or must tunnel repeatedly through transverse ridges.

This alternative plan, which can be put into a space about two and a half by seven times the minimum radius used, has the advantage of exposing a greater percentage of the track to view. For a convincing effect, though, the steeply graded end loops must be concealed, with the hidden portions at least as long as a train. The hills covering the end loops should be high so as to "frame" the picture. Electrically speaking, this layout also does not have a reversing loop unless a crossover between the mainline tracks is added.

Look around on your favorite railroad—chances are that there is at least one place on its line already "pretwisted" so that you can fit it neatly into your available space and create a stage across which your prize rolling stock can parade in all its glory, with the loops and cutoffs that got it there out of sight and out of mind.

Modeling the White Pass & Yukon

A fascinating railroad is the proud WP&Y. It can be condensed into a narrow or standard gauge model layout that will effectively portray the rugged drama of railroading

AT BEST, a model railroad is somewhat of a caricature of a conventional prototype line. The curves are too sharp, the trains and the main line are too short, and the changes in scenery from one section to another are too abrupt. As a railroad, it's a strange one. Truth may be stranger than fiction, though, so perhaps we should look for a real road whose "strangeness" with respect to the usual railroad is such as to make it more like the typical home pike, and use it for a prototype. We may come closer to reality than by dreaming up a wholly fictional track plan of a more conventional railroad, and there's an answer for the skeptic who says, "You mean there's a prototype for that?"

Such a line whose nature meets halfway the needs of the practical track plan is the White Pass & Yukon, a three-foot gauge line still very much in business between Skagway, Alaska, and Whitehorse, Yukon Territory. Its curves are too sharp (16 to 24 degrees); a 3.9 per cent ruling grade keeps its trains short; its surrounding scenery is space-savingly vertical and changes character with model-like abruptness in crossing timberline twice in a few miles. Yet it's a real railroad which proudly does a man-size job and sticks strictly to big-time operating practice wherever it doesn't conflict with the peculiar problems of its traffic, terrain, and climate.

In this chapter, therefore, we'll try to capture some of the operating spirit and some of the scenic highlights of this aggressive little road in a practical layout. In the basic plan, the most scenic and heavily traveled section of the WP&Y from Skagway to Carcross is represented in a track plan scaled for O3 gauge in a space equivalent to one-half of a two-car garage. With equipment constructed to the O gauge scale of ¼" to the foot, the track gauge becomes equal to that of standard OO gauge.

Our WP&Y track plan is strictly point to point. As we shall see, the rugged terrain spanned by the prototype results in a lot of railroading to handle even light traffic, so there's no need in the model to make it easy to send the same train scurrying repeat-

---

Author's Insight

The White Pass would have been an irresistible prototype even if I hadn't had the thrill of a 1935 round trip over the whole line. Stretching "Track Plan of the Month" limits, the plan is half-garage size, with an over-hood impingement into the other stall. It's in On3, somewhat of a rarity in the early 1950s but then still perhaps having an edge on scratchbuilding courtesy of any American OO (4 mm scale—¾" gauge) parts still floating around.

Also a bit unusual for that era was its walk-in, once-around design, with a suggestion that all trackage be above hip height, making the aisleway, in effect, wider. Somewhat embarrassing is my reference to the brakeman's "throwing the turnout"—the turnout stays put; what you do throw is the switch, whether point or stub type, as we modelers should remember.

With Sn3 and HOn3 components now available, a smaller-scale version in a similar space, with undiminished aisle width, could stretch siding lengths to handle more typical WP&Y train lengths—strings of up to ten parlor cars and very substantial mixed consists, with ore and container flats behind as many as five six-axle chop-nose Alcos.

The White Pass lives on as far as Bennett as a busy tourist line through the same magnificent scenery. What a prototype!

edly past the same point. By the time you get a tonnage train from Skagway to Carcross, you'll have really seen some action.

At the same time, in the interest of realism of scene, the plan is worked out so that at no point is more than one section of the main line in sight. This is done through use of what might be dubbed the "walk in" type of bench-work arrangement, which has some of the advantages of both the more common "island" and "around the wall" types. There is access to the track at all points and a backdrop behind the main line everywhere it goes, yet you don't have to duck under the layout to follow a train from one end of the line to the other. As in all compact track plans, sections of main line theoretically miles apart are actually close together, but this isn't disconcerting because one section is either on the other side of a backdrop or else behind your back.

To see how the White Pass has been condensed, we can run through a day's operations as they might go on a pike

following the actual road not only in track arrangement and scenic features but in schedules and equipment as well.

For our example, we'll naturally pick a day in summer when a steamer up the Inside Passage from Vancouver or Seattle has brought a shipload of tourists to Skagway. Many of them are going on to Bennett, Whitehorse, or the West Taku Arm, so an additional train is scheduled on ship days.

We find this train has been made up and backed from the Skagway shops yards right down to shipside. Skagway has only 634 population but by gosh it has two places from which passenger trains depart. The West Taku Arm special is double-headed, with a solid consist of wonderful wood open-platform parlor cars, neat but not gaudy in Pullman green with gold lettering. Soon after arrival of the ship it chuffs smartly out of town past the shops, a thin trail of coal smoke streaming from the stovepipe on each car in the crisp morning air.

Action now shifts to the "downtown" station, featuring single track

Men were suspended on ropes to do the initial drilling for the bore through Tunnel Mountain. Rugged scenery makes for interesting modeling.

right down the center of the main drag, where the daily mixed train for Whitehorse is made ready to leave. The street is still unpaved and the wood sidewalks are still there. Most of Skagway consists of buildings dating from the era of the 1898 gold rush to the Klondike.

The Whitehorse train's passenger section, spotted at the station, consists of a flatcar carrying two automobiles (there is no road out of Skagway), a baggage car with regular caboose-style cupola perched atop its monitor roof, a coach and a parlor car with observation end. The railing sports a round wood tail sign proclaiming "Gateway to the Yukon" in bright letters, but which is unlighted since the parlor cars operate only in the summer when at this latitude it never really gets dark. The locomotive is a modern if diminutive Mikado with large tender, front-end throttle, mechanical lubricators, and all

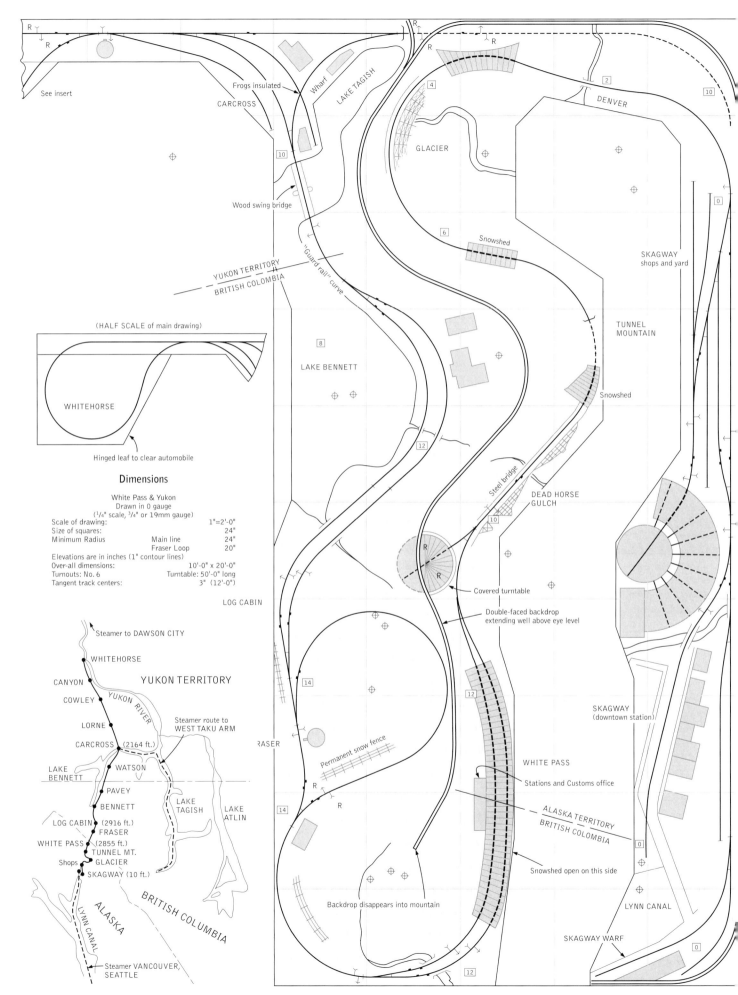

See insert

Frogs insulated

CARCROSS

Wharf

LAKE TAGISH

GLACIER

4

DENVER

2

10

Wood swing bridge

SKAGWAY
shops and yard

"Guard rail" curve

YUKON TERRITORY
BRITISH COLUMBIA

6

Snowshed

TUNNEL
MOUNTAIN

10

(HALF SCALE of main drawing)

8

LAKE BENNETT

Snowshed

WHITEHORSE

12

Steel bridge

DEAD HORSE
GULCH

10

Hinged leaf to clear automobile

Dimensions

White Pass & Yukon
Drawn in O gauge
(¹/₄" scale, ³/₄" or 19mm gauge)

Scale of drawing:	1"=2'-0"
Size of squares:	24"
Minimum Radius Main line	24"
Fraser Loop	20"

Elevations are in inches (1" contour lines)

Over-all dimensions:		10'-0" x 20'-0"
Turnouts: No. 6	Turntable:	50'-0" long
Tangent track centers:		3" (12'-0")

R

R

Covered turntable

Double-faced backdrop
extending well above eye level

LOG CABIN

SKAGWAY
(downtown station)

Steamer to DAWSON CITY

WHITEHORSE

CANYON

COWLEY

YUKON TERRITORY

14

LORNE

YUKON RIVER

Steamer route to
WEST TAKU ARM

12

CARCROSS (2164 ft.)

WATSON

LAKE
BENNETT

PAVEY

FRASER

Permanent snow fence

WHITE PASS

Stations and Customs office

BENNETT

LAKE
TAGISH

LAKE
ATLIN

ALASKA TERRITORY
BRITISH COLOMBIA

LOG CABIN (2916 ft.)

FRASER

14

R

0

WHITE PASS (2855 ft.)

TUNNEL MT.

R

Shops

GLACIER

SKAGWAY (10 ft.)

Snowshed open on this side

BRITISH COLUMBIA

ALASKA

LYNN CANAL

Backdrop disappears into mountain

LYNN CANAL

SKAGWAY WARF

0

Steamer VANCOUVER,
SEATTLE

other up-to-date appliances, plus a very carefully maintained air pump.

The train rolls out of the main street, across a log bridge and up to the shops, where another locomotive is waiting on the main track in the middle of an assortment of loaded freight cars. The passenger section of the train couples onto the freight and a third engine (which in model practice might well be the helper from the preceding passenger train, just returned from the hill) is attached at the head end. The three engines highball off bravely but soon slow to a sedate pace of 12 to 15 m.p.h. as the 3.2 per cent average grade takes hold.

Denver station is one of the easiest modeling jobs on record. It consists solely of a wood sign so inscribed, and that is all—period! Next comes Glacier, a similarly well-populated place at the end of a horseshoe curve, much of which is on a curved wood trestle. The climb continues, reaching a climax at Tunnel Mountain where a rock shelf blasted in the cliff, a trestle, a short rock tunnel, and a timber snowshed follow consecutively.

The train then crosses Steel Bridge, a really impressive structure flanked by two more short, curved wood trestles. It carries the track high above Dead Horse Gulch, named for the thousands of pack animals that died on the slopes of the pass during the gold rush. A covered turntable is on a spur at the upper end of the bridge, and we notice that by now the telegraph poles have been superseded by a cable lying on the ground along the track, recognition of the heavy snowfall along this section of the line.

At White Pass, the track levels off somewhat and enters a snowshed in which the station and customs offices at the international boundary are located. The lead engine and first section of freight cars uncouple and pull ahead on the main while the Canadian officials are checking the passengers, thus releasing the mid-train helper. It backs through the siding to the turntable at Steel Bridge where it is turned for the trip back to Skagway.

The remaining two engines take the train out of White Pass up a continuing grade to Fraser, where the lead engine takes water. We are now on the tracks of the British Columbia Yukon Navigation Co., Ltd. While we were coming up the hill through Alaskan territory we were

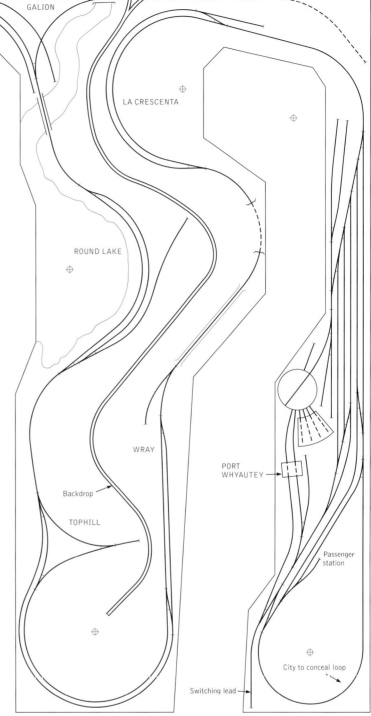

Scale of drawing: 3/8" = 2'-0". Minimum radius, main line: 24"; Port Whyautey loop, 18".

officially on the Pacific and Arctic Railway and Navigation Co., a good West Virginia corporation. It takes three companies as well as three engines to get us from Skagway to Whitehorse, so if you'd like to have a little fun with several subsidiary corporations and the resulting legal complications, even though your pike isn't very long, here's your prototype.

Log Cabin, highest point on the line, is where the second helper, the engine immediately ahead of the passenger cars, is taken out (using the south end of the Bennett siding as a spur track). It backs to Fraser and turns on the loop there for the return to Skagway. Fraser's loop is a necessity for handling the rotary plows which are the line's mainstays in winter. The snow is frequently so deep that even the short backing move, which would be necessary in turning around on a wye, might not be possible.

Bennett consists solely of the station-restaurant and the ruins of a log church,

F. L. JAQUES

from the days when Bennett was the temporary terminus of the railroad. For once it's practicable to model a lineside town in its entirety! About the time we finish lunch, a southbound train pulls in from Carcross, its empty parlor cars being deadheaded back to Skagway to meet tomorrow's ship. The passengers they carried to Carcross this morning are now enjoying a spectacular round trip to the West Taku Arm of Lake Tagish aboard the sternwheeler *Tutshi*, and will return to Skagway on these same cars tomorrow.

As our brakeman throws the turnout to head the southbound train into the siding, we notice that it is a stub switch (as, it turns out, are practically all turnouts on the WP&Y). Under the relatively light traffic they stand up well enough, and they are much to be appreciated in winter since there is no crevice where the snow can collect and keep them from closing. Since our train is considerably longer than the passing track, it is really a saw-by meet as we pull out for Carcross and thus clear the main track for the southbound, but its crew is too busy eating to concern themselves about that.

Next comes Guard Rail Curve, sharpest on the main line, and then a quaint wood gallows-type swing bridge over the Lake Bennett outlet just as the line enters Carcross. This bridge is advertised, perhaps correctly, as the most northerly movable bridge in the world. The train swings to the left at Carcross and there is (for the first time since Skagway) some switching of freight cars in and out of sidings and the wharf track.

Since the line from Carcross on is less spectacular, and space in the garage is

running out, this fifty-mile stretch to Whitehorse has been condensed into a loop, unscenicked so that it can be swung out of the way of the automobile. So, in our model, the train which just left Carcross comes back into view quickly enough to represent its own southbound sister mixed train on the prototype. On the return trip, it will stop for customs at White Pass and will make a few short stops at the most scenic points for the benefit of the camera-carrying passengers and the temperature of the wheel treads and brake shoes.

At the Skagway shops the passenger section of the train is left on the main between the yard switches. The engine then backs through the siding past the train and, leaving the freight cars on the main, pushes the passenger cars the rest of the way down to the station. When you take all day to make 110 miles anyway, there's no need to be in any great rush as far as the passengers are concerned, but the engine, thus kept from being trapped at the end of the single station track, is then available to start switching the freight cars while the express is being unloaded.

One thing missing on the real WP&Y is lineside industry. There is a small tie-treating plant at Carcross, and of course the steamer wharves there and at the terminals, but otherwise there's nothing. This shouldn't stop you from adding a few mines here and there—there's plenty of fool's gold, at least, in them thar hills.

The heated roundhouse at Skagway is a multi-stall affair because virtually all the equipment needed to run the two-trains-per-week minimum winter schedule must be kept indoors between trips.

Now, how about the problems of O3 gauge from the standpoint of actual construction and equipping of a miniature WP&Y? The line is laid with 70-pound rail for the most part, so 125-section S or OO gauge rail, which is equal to 90-pound rail in $\frac{1}{4}''$ scale, is about right especially considering the general tendency to use rail slightly heavier than prototype in scale modeling practice. Ties are about 7 feet long, so S gauge nine-footers are within three scale inches of being on the nose. Incidentally, while the White Pass main isn't supported by 5 feet of rock ballast like the Norfolk & Western, the track is well maintained, particularly on the hill, and boasts tie plates on curves. While the White Pass companies are British-owned, roadway and equipment are strictly American style.

As far as motive power goes, WP&Y depends on three classes of modern Mikes (with frames between the drivers as on standard gauge engines), a venerable outside-frame Ten-Wheeler and one outside-frame Consolidation.

The passenger rolling stock is distinctive, to say the least, particularly in its two-to-one ratio of parlor cars to coaches. The cars are short (about 48 feet), low-slung, and all beautifully maintained. Two ex-Sumpter Valley (Oregon) combines have been fitted with cupolas to team with the two similarly-equipped baggage cars in eliminating the need for a separate caboose on mixed trains. It is a law that there be an observation point on trains carrying freight cars.

Freight cars are from 24 to 30 feet long and include all standard types. Since there is no other road connecting with the WP&Y onto which they might

Above left: Shipside scene gives the modeler an excellent opportunity to get away from the conventional and frequently overdone effects of a "landlocked" railroad. A well-maintained parlor car, typical of the equipment of proud WP&Y, has lines that would impart to a model that extra bit of authenticity.

Above: Two flatcars loaded with automobiles point up the fact that WP&Y is the only means of transportation between Skagway and Carcross. Because it hauls in all basic needs of its on-line communities, WP&Y retains nearly all of its original "golden age of railroading" atmosphere.

Above right: Skagway shops present an array of weathered wood structures that would add character to any model pike. Forested slopes in background present a contrast to the clutter of buildings, stub switches, and wobbly tracks—a point worth remembering when modeling a scene like this.

Rigid rails

Fins

Insulating gaps

Spring loaded to normal route

Sheet brass fin soldered in tight-fitting slot in movable rail

Make this slot in rigid rail large enough to enable fin to move freely

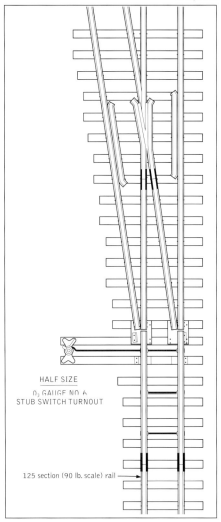

HALF SIZE

O3 GAUGE NO. 6
STUB SWITCH TURNOUT

125 section (90 lb. scale) rail

wander, most of them are devoid of identification except for the number. OO gauge trucks will do; S gauge trucks equipped with OO wheels and an appropriately shortened bolster would be a little closer to correct scale. Standard automatic couplers are used (about S gauge in size) but all are still fitted with a slot for link and pin.

How about building this layout in HO3? It can be done, all right, but because of the walk-in feature the layout will not shrink in proportion. In general, HO gaugers are not markedly different in personal girth from those who favor the bigger scales.

On the other hand, if this general plan is built to the same actual size in HO standard gauge, retaining the same siding lengths, it becomes typical of a heavy-duty single-track line plagued with a tough climb over a coastal range into the interior. The Port Whyautey Midland is the same track plan as the WP&Y except that, in keeping with the needs of heavier traffic, a loop has been provided at the port end. The same scenic ideas as in the White Pass apply; operations are similar to those on the Convolutions & Western (July '52 MR), but incomparably more realistic because they have been spread out in five times the space.

The White Pass & Yukon happens to be unusually adaptable to modeling, but whatever your taste in prototypes, don't overlook the advantages in realism that can come from a careful study of a real railroad and its adaptation to your space.

The Mighty Bantam

Even long, articulated-hauled freights can operate

realistically on layouts too small for anything but bantam

curves if certain design principles are used.

CAN THE following specifications for a track plan be met without losing most of the realism of first-class scale model railroading?

(1) A line on which an articulated can operate, hauling freights that look appropriate to its bulk.
(2) Some passenger operation, not with streamlined equipment, but not a doodle-bug operation either.
(3) Over-all size—4 x 8 feet in HO or its equivalent in other scales.

That last requirement puts the hooker in it! Well, it isn't impossible, but it will take a little review of the basic facts on track curvature, and a willingness to go in for careful layout construction with a few refinements not always used these days. Also, many alternate operating features will have to be relinquished-but here goes.

Articulateds are being built these days that will take bantam (18″ in HO, 36″ in O) curves. As far as passenger service is concerned, there are plenty of non-freak 65-foot steam road prototype cars around the country, so with a proper choice of conditions we may be able to get something reasonable in this department, too. Let's take up some ideas that apply and see, one by one, how they are used in the 4 x 8-foot Nasmyth & Lake Michigan.

USE TRANSITION CURVES – THEY'RE A SPACE BARGAIN

In any kind of model railroading, our curves are way too sharp. I remember that once on an O gauge club layout we had as our pride and joy a curve, somewhat more than a semicircle in extent, of 12-foot radius! It was something to see—trains really looked at home as they rolled smoothly around its gentle arc. Yet, in the civil engineer's system of measuring the sharpness of a curve by the amount it turns in 100 feet of track, this was a 10 degree curve, and the Pennsy's horseshoe curve, the time-honored standard for prototype sharp-ness in the curve department, rates only 9¼ degrees.

So our curves are always too severe. The question is: Just how severe a curve can we stand? Excessive curvature

── *Author's Insight* ──

How about running an HO standard gauge drag rating an articulated locomotive and a local passenger on a 4 x 8 layout? That was the challenge which brought forth a line so compact that it depends for any degree of realism on representing a line like the Escanaba & Lake Superior, carrying iron ore down to a port; a railroad owned by a steel company, like the Bessemer & Lake Erie, presumably takes over at the receiving end of the voyage. Sir Henry Bessemer is memorialized as the inventor of the iron-to-steel conversion process; Joseph Nasmyth rates recognition as the inventor of the steam hammer that has pounded so much steel into side rods, so we have our Nasmyth & Lake Michigan.

So much for the name—meeting the space with something that will stay within the limits of reasonable appearance calls for such moderately advanced features such as eased curves, no.5 and curved turnouts, and tinkered-with tender-truck pivot locations, some of which in turn call for the fairly detailed explanations making up the bulk of the text.

Cramped as it is, the N&LM has one curve of prototypical gentleness. It has been introduced purely to make a train on it look more authentically interesting than it would on a straightaway in the same space—what we'd now call a "cosmetic" curve.

WILLIAM D. MIDDLETON

Duluth, Missabe & Iron Range Ry. M4 class 2-8-8-4 no. 228 waits in the Fraser, Minnesota, yard with a 190-car ore extra.

causes trouble in operating reliability and appearance. Considerable progress has been made in developing equipment that can in some fashion get around a bantam curve or one even sharper, and most of the deviations from strict scale which are incorporated in the NMRA standards, such as oversize wheel flanges, are basically concessions to the need for reasonably compact model railroads. Other things being equal, a successful pike in the smallest sizes must depend on excellent trackwork, well maintained, to overcome even partially the handicap of excessively sharp curves.

Appearance-wise, trains don't look too good just standing on sharply curved track. It's that lurch as the cars

enter a curve, though, that changes what should be the smooth gliding of a serpent-like train into something more like the amusement park Whip. Here is where you can use a device that prototype roads, with their vastly broader curves, still find essential. The "transition curve," "spiral," or "easement" is a section of track of gradually increasing curvature joining tangent track to the body of the curve which is of constant radius. In fig. 1 we see what even a short easement can do in de-lurching 65-foot cars as they enter sharp curves. From the lurch standpoint, the bantam curve with easement is considerably better than the conventional curve without. If our equipment will take the sharper curve at all, we can actually get

smoother operation and better appearance with the smaller radius. There is some space used up by the offset between the tangent and the arc of the curve, but a 180 degree curve can still be made in a total width (in HO, for example) of 36¾" instead of 48".

It goes without saying that you're still better off with a larger radius curve and an easement. The old NMRA standard minimum radii are still what we should use wherever possible. But using too big a radius may result in a poorer plan if you are fitting a pike into a space that has been established by

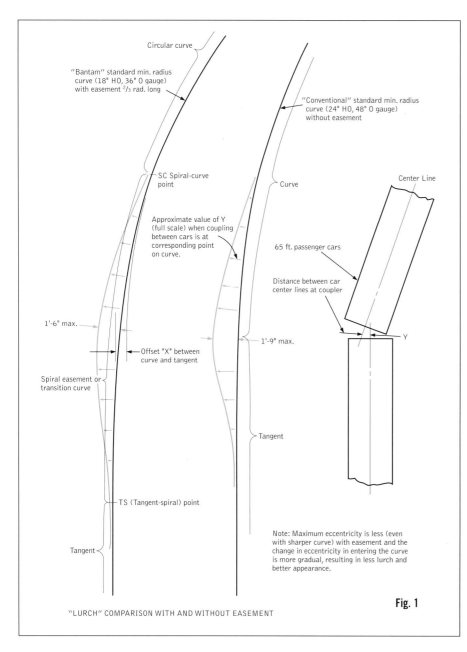

Circular curve

"Bantam" standard min. radius curve (18" HO, 36" O gauge) with easement ²/₃ rad. long

"Conventional" standard min. radius curve (24" HO, 48" O gauge) without easement

SC Spiral-curve point

Curve

Center Line

Approximate value of Y (full scale) when coupling between cars is at corresponding point on curve.

65 ft. passenger cars

Distance between car center lines at coupler

1'-6" max.

Offset "X" between curve and tangent

1'-9" max.

Y

Spiral easement or transition curve

TS (Tangent-spiral) point

Tangent

Tangent

Tangent

Note: Maximum eccentricity is less (even with sharper curve) with easement and the change in eccentricity in entering the curve is more gradual, resulting in less lurch and better appearance.

Fig. 1

"LURCH" COMPARISON WITH AND WITHOUT EASEMENT

some higher authority (such as the rest of the family) as all that will ever be available. There will be too little straight track and the general scheme may have to be simplified to the point of being uninteresting just to get the broad curves into the limited space. Insurance is a prudent investment, but you can go broke by buying too much of it; broad curves are somewhat the same.

The N&LM plan this month is drawn with easement on all mainline curves to show how they affect a layout. Just keep in mind that any plan given here can be adapted to easements by reducing the radius slightly (about 1" in O, ½" in HO) to take care of the offset distance x.

Isn't an easement a hard thing to use and beyond the powers of the average toiler in the vineyard of prefabricated

track and jiffy kits? Not necessarily. Figure 2 gives one of several methods. Other methods range up to actual calculations, using a civil engineering text on railway curves and earthwork. An excellent dissertation on the subject will be found in NMRA data sheet D3c which appeared in 1952. Just try one easement and the results will make you love 'em, even if they are a little more work.

USE A VARIETY OF TURNOUTS, INCLUDING CURVED ONES

One of the stunts we're using in the N&LM to meet that stingy space allotment is to make it an iron ore road using 24-foot cars. Boy, are they space savers-they're even shorter than a Sierra combine! Since they'll go around super-substandard curves when not coupled

to longer equipment, we use no. 3 turnouts where only the real "stumpies" are used; Out on the line, though, the no. 4 turnouts usually associated with bantam curvature aren't quite enough to handle the articulated and the passenger cars, so we use 5s and 6s where there's room. You can't buy a no. 5? Well, that's too bad, because it's a mighty useful size in places where a no. 4 is too short and a no. 6 too long. The N&LM is drawn up so that standard 6s can be substituted for the 5s (with some loss of siding capacity) if you don't want to try your hand at building the odd size.

Curved switches? Somebody said a naughty word! True, a curved turnout is to be avoided if it isn't necessary, but the space saving is such that we can't get by without a few of them here if siding lengths are to be kept adequate for our articulated-hauled trains. For example, where our main line comes up the hill into the principal terminal of Nasmyth, we can increase the capacity of our run-around track by about three cars by starting the switch on the easement. A special turnout, built up to fit and with a curved frog, would be the ultimate, but a very satisfactory approximation can be made. Take a standard no. 8 turnout (kit or pre-assembled), loosen the rails from the clips on one side, and bend the whole shebang until the track that was straight now conforms to the easement curve at that particular point. With fiber tie strip, it may be necessary to clip the strip connecting the ties on one side to give enough flexibility. All the other curved turnouts can be similarly constructed from either no. 6 or no. 8 standards.

After you've laid out the theoretical curve as carefully as possible, sight along the tracks as they are spiked down and smooth out visible kinks with the hammer and nail set. This is a necessary step in any special trackwork. If you're building a road like this in HO, you have only 32 square feet of pike to build, so you can afford to be careful with the details.

Perhaps it's time now to see what the basic plan of the N&LM is. Its job is to get ore from the mines of upper Michigan and wheel it down to the lake boats, and Nasmyth is its upper terminal. Here mine runs bring in loads from the Narco pit and presumably from other nearby mines not shown. The cars are sorted out here by composition to make a properly balanced blast furnace

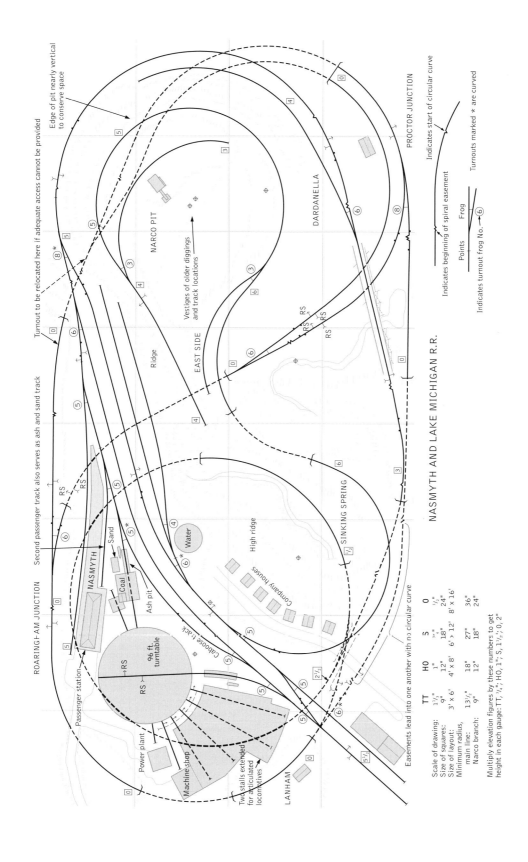

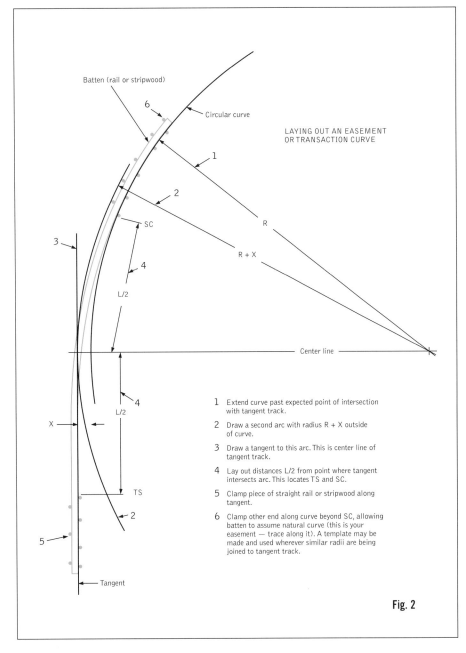

Batten (rail or stripwood)

Circular curve

LAYING OUT AN EASEMENT
OR TRANSACTION CURVE

6

1

2

SC

3

4

R

R + X

L/2

4

L/2

X

TS

5

Tangent

Center line

1 Extend curve past expected point of intersection with tangent track.

2 Draw a second arc with radius R + X outside of curve.

3 Draw a tangent to this arc. This is center line of tangent track.

4 Lay out distances L/2 from point where tangent intersects arc. This locates TS and SC.

5 Clamp piece of straight rail or stripwood along tangent.

6 Clamp other end along curve beyond SC, allowing batten to assume natural curve (this is your easement — trace along it). A template may be made and used wherever similar radii are being joined to tangent track.

Fig. 2

charge after the loads are mixed in loading the ore boat at the docks. Solid train-loads then drift gingerly down the steadily descending main line to the docks. On the trip back up the ore cars are empty. Joined by a few inbound cars of miscellaneous freight for the mining communities, they are still a heavy enough load, considering the steady grade, to require big engines.

Helpers, though, are the exception rather than the rule. At Nasmyth, empties for the Narco pit are taken in hand by the mining company's switchers for the trip to the diggings. With the short tail track and the switchback siding to the loading site, considerable scurrying back and forth between the pit and East Side is necessary to get all the

empties back to the shovel and the loads on the mine branch ready to be pushed to Nasmyth. The basic main line plan is an out-and-back, or rather a down-and-back, with the single terminal at a high elevation. The main line actually spirals down to an oval (reaching it at Lanham) where trains may indulge in continuous running if desired. A trip through the Roaringham Junction-Proctor Junction connection turns them around ready for the return. There is a train-length passing track, mostly concealed, on the lower level, but for the most part the N&LM doesn't feature tricky single-track operation with frequent meets and passes—there isn't room for much of that when you concentrate on the

arrangements necessary for relatively long trains.

Passenger service is furnished by a single train of two to four cars hauled by a tough, low-wheeled Ten-Wheeler or Pacific with enough dig to make smooth starts on the continuously ascending grade. Two or three round trips a day are run. If you want to offer sleeper service on the early morning run up from the lake with connection from Chicago or Duluth, a railroad operated coach-sleeper with six sections or so at one end would be in keeping with the flavor of the road, and its length could be held to the 65-foot limit without violating prototype.

The passenger train pulls into its own track at Nasmyth and sits there panting while the head-end traffic is unloaded. The gentle curve on which it rests illustrates another small-pike principle: Every layout, no matter how small, is entitled to ONE prototype-radius curve.

This track could have been straight, but by curving it at a very large radius we have at least one place on the layout where equipment can be seen (and photographed) in a completely scale setting. Similarly, since there is nothing to be gained by a short radius, the curve in the middle of the yard is made relatively gentle, with a radius two or three times the minimum used on the rest of the line.

The thought of big engines on sharp curves brings up two other points. One is that it is at least as legitimate to modify (in an invisible way) a piece of rolling stock to obtain good appearance as it is to tinker with it (by removing flanges, etc.) to get it to negotiate excessively sharp curves. As fig. 3 shows, Pacifies don't look too good on sharp bends, but some kingpin relocation can help considerably.

Secondly, the reminder to "watch the overhanging end" is as essential in connection with an articulated as it was on those old streetcars with the long platforms. At Dardanella we have put the siding on the inside of the curve so that when the articulated with its train on the main line meets the passenger train which is in the siding (standard operating practice for an ore road), there will be no scraping sounds. The passing track at Proctor Junction is too sharp for the big fellow. He must always take the outer track, so the between-track clearance there need only be enough for the second largest engine on the line. If you

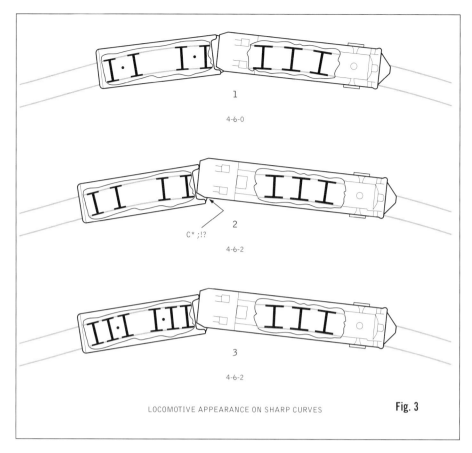

1. Locomotives without trailing trucks, and therefore with short overhang behind the rear drivers, are best for short radii, appearance-wise. Note that the cab and tender of this 4-6-0 are still pretty much in line on a bantam curve.

2. The cab of this Pacific swings way out and exposes the front inside corner of the tender. This not only results in an ungainly appearance, but also tends to foul the drawbar, causing derailments and rough running.

3. Considerable improvement can be made by moving kingpins back on tender trucks. This causes the tender to swing outwards, thereby resulting in better alignment of tender and locomotive cab. This kingpin relocation is even more effective on tenders with four-wheel trucks.

4-6-0

C* ;!?

2

4-6-2

3

4-6-2

LOCOMOTIVE APPEARANCE ON SHARP CURVES

Fig. 3

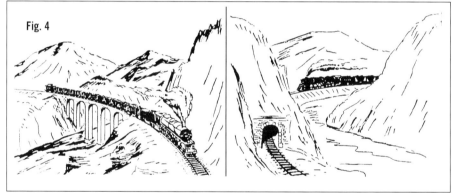

Fig. 4

Something doesn't look right in the left-hand picture. That articulated is much too heavy for such a short train. How can we overcome this unrealistic effect? Well, we can plan our scenery to hide part of the train from view at all times, as in the right-hand picture. The length of the train is not so noticeable, thereby giving an appearance that is much closer to prototype.

have two articulateds, I'll bet you're not in the market for a 4 x 8-ft. railroad.

Scenically, a high ridge down the center of the layout will tend to help by dividing the pike into two separate areas—the Nasmyth terminal and town and the Narco pit scene—neither of which is too badly overcrowded. Otherwise, there are the usual minor inconsistencies in the scenery that require some alibi artistry. Since it seems a shame to cover up the entire spiral that the main line uses to gain elevation, a piece of it has been left visible in a narrow gorge.

This introduces drainage problems which could only be solved by assuming an unusual, if not unheard of, natural phenomenon and naming the place Sinking Spring. Maybe it should be made into a state park.

The reason for some of the other interruptions to the visibility of the main line is explained in fig. 4. We can readily run trains of about 16 or 17 of our 18-to-the-dozen short ore hoppers, but even that would look like a puny load for a Challenger if it all could be seen at once.

It takes easements, curved turnouts,

elimination of some types of operating possibilities, and painstaking construction to do it, but the Nasmyth & Lake Michigan can give fairly realistic passenger and big-power operation in 4 x 8 feet. Maybe some of the tricks employed will help you out in less cramped over-ambitious situations.

Cajon Pass in Your Garage

The excitement of dispatching trains over one of the

West's most famous passes can be yours – in HO – if you've

a 10 x 20-foot space in which you can build this layout,

complete with authentic, spectacular scenery.

LAYOUT SPACE is where you find it, and no serious model railroader will let the fact that garages are intended as storage areas for automobiles keep him from contemplating the type of pike which could be put into a clear space 10 x 20 feet or thereabouts.

Once you've satisfied yourself that the garage is the most likely spot, there's just one fundamental decision to make: Can you get away with booting the car out into the driveway permanently? Climate, domestic relations, car age and at-work parking conditions must be considered, along with all-night parking restrictions in some cities. (Actually, any 10 x 20-foot space will suit the plan we're going to develop, so if you can't steal the garage, maybe you can get away with a similar area in your basement.)

After you make the big decision and banish the car from its home for keeps,

a great set of opportunities opens up. The 200 square feet or so available is enough for a full scenic treatment and decently long straightaways. Might as well step right in and try for the works: a mainline-type pike with a good-sized yard, full operating possibilities, and scenery based on some real-life territory of unusual railroad interest. Then you'll have something really worthwhile to make up for all the explaining as to why your new car sits outdoors.

Biting off a big chunk, let's try Cajon Pass, the "big hill of Southern California," where Santa Fe and Union Pacific trains climb 2700 feet in 25 miles amid scenery of real grandeur. As fig. 1 shows, we have from San Bernardino to Summit a stretch of double track including a switchover to left-hand operation, a yard with major shops, two separate tracks much of the way, tunnels (nice if we need them for folding our track up

into the space and hiding just what goes on), and a swift transition between two varieties of scenery. Just what the doctor ordered–leave us proceed!

As a little controlled doodling in the 2 x 4-square space of our garage shows (fig. 2), with the conventional-radius curves (HO) we need for mainline equipment it's going to be hard to get

Author's Insight

Apart from simply not providing continuing operating interest (or, to be a bit irreverent, "play value") over the years, faults most likely to cause abandonment of a layout seem to be those related to poor access for operation, viewing, and maintenance. Unreachable turnouts, duck- or even crawl-unders are continuing irritants; among the worst are those hard-to-conceal access hatches—lids requiring a long-armed second person to hold the blamed things up if cherished nearby scenery is not to be destroyed. Most desirable, of course, is a walk-in aisle configuration with all vital elements within reach.

As a modelable location, Cajon Pass has everything: two

busy railroads operating over a crucial ruling grade through a rugged and—most time-, cost-, and effort-saving—largely treeless terrain adjoining the track and facilities of a division point. As illustrated, however, best squeezing this into a one-stall garage calls for a doughnut configuration, accepting the lesser nuisance of drop-leaf entry. Spectacular geography allows adequate occasional from-below access at all critical points without too much exaggeration of reality.

This compromise has yielded a track plan that has remained popular while accommodating everything from heavyweight Pullmans to Superliners and small 2-10-2s to Dash 9s.

ROBERT HALE

adequate space for operating the pike and watching the trains without a duck-under. (See the Jan. '56 MR, page 51 for an explanation of "controlled doodling" as used to figure roughly what arrangements are possible in a given space.) Ten feet just isn't quite enough width. A drawbridge being a little out of the question in our territory (though it might be nice to have in the prototype when those flash floods come through), we reluctantly settle for a central access space with a drop-leaf carrying a couple of tracks across the entryway, as in fig. 2 (D). This trades a little inconvenience for a much-improved appearance in which the same train doesn't get quite so tangled up in its own tracks in making one circuit of the main line.

CAJON PASS IN MINIATURE

Starting at the somewhat accursed drop-leaf, we find in the final plan that just as in Los Angeles country, trains can come into San Berdoo from two lines of the Santa Fe (the second division from L.A. via Pasadena or the third subdivision via Fullerton) and the UP connection at Riverside. This double-barrelled arrangement allows us to have two good train hideaways under the main area of the layout with the fewest possible concealed turnouts. If the optional crossover indicated is added, we can be correct in always having UP trains travel on the proper route, while the Santa Fe traffic is divided between the two subdivisions.

San Berdoo yard is a major classification point for the Santa Fe, where the heavy traffic originating along the lines from L.A. and several branches is consolidated with the consists from the city itself to make up the fruit blocks, merchandise manifests, and inevitably, trains of empties, for movement to the

Top of Cajon Pass (pronounced Ca-hone) is at Summit, California. Unusual details here that offer interesting modeling possibilities are the cluster of small service buildings around the station, the houses and barracks-type living quarters for railroad employees, the small wood water tank, and the turning wye for helper engines.

eastward. The motive power picture can be varied as you like by shifts of only a few years in time; Cajon has been dieselized not once but several times as traffic rushes, slow deliveries of new units, and changes in motive power department ideas have conspired to send the steamers back onto the Hill after they were declared officially dead. So, we'll naturally pick a time, say the late '40s, when steam was still basic on both roads.

Not too long before that, both lines used the big Santa Fe roundhouse which we duplicate in principle with

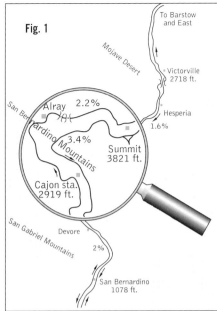

Fig. 1

To Barstow and East

Mojave Desert

Victorville 2718 ft.

San Bernardino Mountains

Alray 2.2%

Hesperia

1.6%

3.4%

Summit 3821 ft.

Cajon sta. 2919 ft.

San Gabriel Mountains

Devore

2%

San Bernardino 1078 ft.

A track-level view of Summit, a lonely spot 3,283 feet above sea level.

our eight-stall job. Later, the UP built its own smaller house across the tracks, but that's a bit out of the question in our space. Most unique feature of the engine terminal is its pony-truss turntable—not so good for showing off locomotives perhaps, but a gem to model in its own right.

Behind the five tracks of the freight yard lie the passenger facilities—three through tracks with railhead-height platforms and a large mission-style station housing the Santa Fe's Los Angeles Division offices. Most trains merely pause here for minor servicing and handling passenger and head-end traffic, but the Santa Fe usually manages to have some equipment parked on the station tracks, and you may feel that the optional passenger setout tracks by the station are worth what they cost in reduced room for a partially three-dimensional background scene. It's unfortunate that we have to locate the passenger facilities at the rear of the platform, where they're not as visible as we'd like. The usual procedure in this case would be to elevate them a little, but the San Berdoo yards are just about as near to perfect flatness as any I've seen, so a compromise is to locate the entire yard a bit lower than usual—say about 38″ or 40″ above the floor—and superdetail the roofs of your passenger cars. In view of the mountains to come, the low base elevation won't hurt the pike as a whole.

At Fifth Street Tower all trains cross over from the previously right-hand operation and start uphill on the left main track. Passenger trains, unless hauled by three or four diesel units totaling 6000 h.p., are double-headed, and freights require one or two helpers.

The grade, 2.8 per cent in our case to better simulate the drag of the 2.2 per cent prototype on train tonnage ratings, begins right at the yard limit and continues uninterruptedly to Summit. At first, through Devore, the track is straight as the line climbs the alluvial fan of gravel issuing from the valley between the San Gabriel and San Bernardino mountains. Then comes Cajon station, a crossing of the normally dry Cajon Creek, and a succession of sweeping curves to the top. Our eastbound, left-hand track swings away to the left through Alray, and the reason for the reverse operation becomes clear. The right-hand track is shorter but correspondingly steeper, and hence is used only by downhill traffic; the more favorable eastward track was the second to be constructed and could only be located to the left of the original.

Alray siding is a miserable place to stop a tonnage train for the passing of a streamliner, so the dispatcher will ordinarily hold freights in the yard for a clear shot at the summit. Often, though, traffic is too heavy for this, so the rails of the passing track stay shiny. The turnout at the uphill end of Alray siding poses an access problem: In making our scene impressive in its extent, we have a platform almost 6 feet wide, and

covered with scenery that could only with difficulty be made stout enough to stand on. Mike and Ike came to the rescue, though. They are a pair of gigantic rock formations featured in so many of the classic action photos of trains climbing Cajon. By leaving their plaster counterparts open at the rear, as in fig. 3, it is possible to get to such remote potential trouble spots from below, and the day is saved.

SUMMIT ACTION

Still taking the long route, the uphill track swings close to the westbound main beyond Alray and then away again to the left. Two short tunnels follow and then at Summit the tracks come back together for good. The freights continue on the level track until the caboose (if it's a Santa Fe drag, you really should call it a way car) clears the short spur coming in from the left. The helper engines cut off from the train, back the caboose up the steep grade of the spur, pull forward again, leaving it there, and then back along the main track to clear the turnout. The road crewmen then let gravity roll the crummy down against the train, brakes are tested, and the freight is ready to proceed on its downhill way. Meanwhile the helpers turn on the wye, couple up with any other engines that may be waiting there after pusher duty, and return to the foot of the hill when traffic permits.

Beyond Summit our remaining trackage is primarily concerned with getting

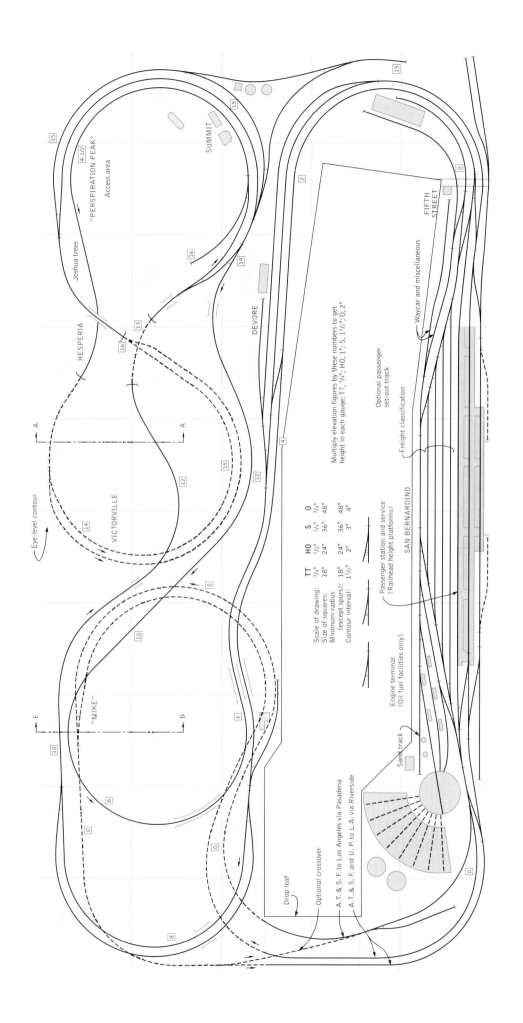

"PERSPIRATION PEAK"

4-1/2"

Access area

SUMMIT

Joshua trees

HESPERIA

DEVORE

Eye-level contour

A — A

VICTORVILLE

"MIKE"

E

B

Drop leaf

Optional crossover

A.T. & S. F. to Los Angeles via Pasadena

A.T. & S. F. and U. P. to L.A. via Riverside

Sand track

Engine terminal
(Oil fuel facilities only)

SAN BERNARDINO

Passenger station and service
(Railhead height platforms)

Freight classification

Optional passenger
set-out track

Waycar and miscellaneous

FIFTH
STREET

Multiply elevation figures by these numbers to get
height in each gauge: TT, 3/4"; HO, 1"; S, 1 1/2"; 0, 2"

	TT	HO	S	0
Scale of drawing:	3/4"	1/2"	1/8"	3/4"
Size of squares:	18"	24"	36"	48"
Minimum radius (except spurs):	18"	24"	36"	48"
Contour interval:	1 1/2"	2"	3"	4"

trains turned around to provide the heavy flow of traffic that's a hallmark of the Pass. At Hesperia we simulate the overhead crossing (actually near Victorville in the prototype, but we don't have 20 miles available) that returns trains to right-hand operation. Although it should be out of sight behind the mountain range, we leave a gap through which this spot of interest can be seen. It's definitely the Mojave Desert back there, with Joshua trees to emphasize its distance from the foreground.

Victorville loop, with its layover siding so trains can come back in different sequence from their disappearances, is actually above the uphill line at two points, but concealed by some of the many ridges and hummocks in which this territory fortunately abounds. The trick is to cover this symmetrical loop with irregular terrain so it isn't obvious what's being hidden, as though a piece of rope were merely covered with a rug. Access is important here too, and again (fig. 4) the height of the mountains allows you to get at important hidden trackage and turnouts without hatches or other visible breaks in the scenery. Clearances are close between track levels at places, requiring careful construction and accurate calculation of grades. But make no mistake—this is an advanced type of layout in which the not inconsiderable problems of construction are balanced out by the satisfaction in having as an end product a real creation in both scenic and operating realism and interest.

Puffing back up the lighter grade into Summit from the east, our freights can take siding while passenger trains pass them and head down the 4 per cent. The time's not wasted, for the brakemen must turn up the air brake retainers on a good proportion of the cars, even with dynamic-brake diesels. The siding at Devore is also a place in which a freight can stop without particular regret, since wheels must be cooled there for 10 minutes in any event. Because of our somewhat limited space for crossovers at Fifth Street, though, downhill freights which are to enter the yard at San Berdoo should take the right-hand track at Devore so they can head directly into the ladder track. In any case, there's no doubt on our return to the busy packing sheds, prosperous citrus and walnut groves and Mediterranean climate of the lowland area that we have covered a lot of ground as far as scenic variation, railroad engi-

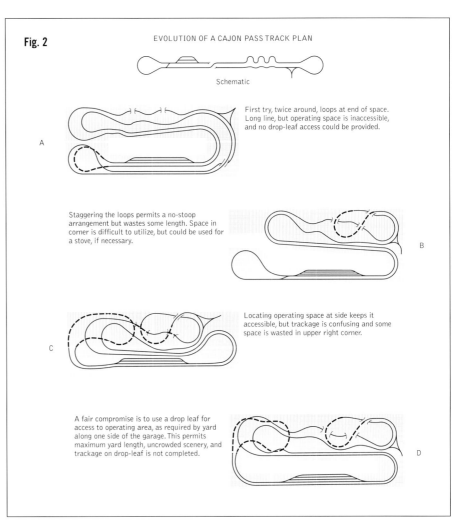

EVOLUTION OF A CAJON PASS TRACK PLAN

Fig. 2

Schematic

A — First try, twice around, loops at end of space. Long line, but operating space is inaccessible, and no drop-leaf access could be provided.

B — Staggering the loops permits a no-stoop arrangement but wastes some length. Space in corner is difficult to utilize, but could be used for a stove, if necessary.

C — Locating operating space at side keeps it accessible, but trackage is confusing and some space is wasted in upper right corner.

D — A fair compromise is to use a drop leaf for access to operating area, as required by yard along one side of the garage. This permits maximum yard length, uncrowded scenery, and trackage on drop-leaf is not completed.

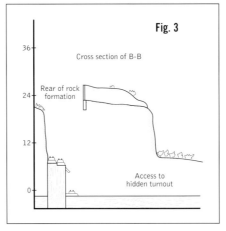

Fig. 3

Cross section of B-B

Rear of rock formation

Access to hidden turnout

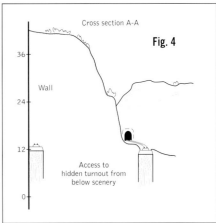

Cross section A-A

Fig. 4

Wall

Access to hidden turnout from below scenery

neering and genuine operating problems are concerned, and in the space of a one-stall garage.

One of the more satisfactory aspects of modeling a widely publicized section of railroad is the abundance of material available to help you make a faithful reproduction of the area and to operate it realistically, even if you can't visit it often or at all. Cajon Pass has been covered in articles in Oct. '41, April and June '47, Sept. '51, and May '54 issues of

Trains, with many individual pictures of Cajon scenes in other issues. From these you learn such useful tidbits as the fact that block signals on the uphill line display a yellow signal behind an ascending train—no need to worry about being unable to stop short of a train on that grade, and stopping any train unnecessarily is a thing to be avoided, so no red aspect is provided.

Selection of a line used by trains of more than one railroad is also a good

The Cajon Pass region has sparse vegetation that's easy to model. The east slope has joshua trees.

gimmick, even if you are using fictional road names. Because of the two roads lifting their trains over Cajon's hump, its rocky gorges resounded in steam's heyday to the exhaust of engines of 4-6-2, 4-10-2, 2-8-2, 2-10-2, 4-8-4, 2-8-8-0, and 4-6-6-4 wheel arrangements as a routine diet—what more could even a model railroad club ask for in the way of justification for variety! Finally, whether you think of Southern California as the Garden of Eden or as a hopeless jungle of 20-lane freeways going nowhere and lost in smog, its countryside has two wonderful advantages for modeling purposes: sparse, easily reproduced vegetation you can afford; and rocky ground which provides prototypes for the steeply sloped cuts, gorges, and ridges we so desperately need as space savers.

Massive, spectacular rock formations near Cajon, a trademark of the pass, are called Ike and Mike.

The Case for Nonbranching

Branch lines don't always wander off into the weeds

away from the main line. Sometimes they're built right

alongside the high iron – and with good reason, too!

A FEW thoughtful and heroic souls will base their pikes on secondary trackage—a branch of a mainline railroad or perhaps the wiggly iron of a short line outfit—and reap the benefit of being able to reproduce realistically the short trains, small yards, and casual operation typical of their chosen prototype. The rest of us will remain unable to ignore the glamour of the high iron and will first insist on wrapping a main line around our available space, fitting a branch in later.

Well, that makes pretty good sense too. Having both big-time and jerkwater railroading in one track plan gives reason for using both extremes of the conglomeration of large and small motive power with which most of us somehow seem to end up, helps account for the typical confusion of road names on our engines and cars, and enhances the variety that is the strongest point of the hobby.

The rub is that the typical branch line in reality does just those things most inconvenient or least profitable to model correctly in a limited space. Since its reason for being is to tap otherwise bypassed territory, a branch naturally takes off in a direction roughly at right angles to the main line; such space as we are likely to be able to allocate for a spur line is almost invariably going to be alongside at least one of the loops of the already cramped main line. Main lines tend to follow the valleys, so branches usually head uphill from the junction point, often with spectacular grades. Our branches are so short, though, that they usually don't provide reasonable excuse for helper engine operation and the other aspects of mountain grades that make for a fascinating layout.

There's a 7.8-mile line in western New York, however, that inspires a useful variation on the "main line plus branch" theme. Look at the Dansville & Mount Morris on a flat map and you'll wonder how it can survive. Its main line extends from a connection with the Lackawanna at Groveland Station to Dansville, a town of 5000 which is also right on the same Lackawanna main stem! A contour map clears up some of the mystery. It seems that the relatively easy going across the Lake Ontario watershed comes to an end for the Lackawanna at Groveland and then begins a steady ascent along the side of

Author's Insight

There's nothing like a branch or connecting short line to add operating variety to a layout, however condensed, that is based on Class I railroading. This article latches onto a real, if rare, alignment as inspiration for dodging the fact that branches typically head off uphill into new territory at an angle to the main—just what we equally typically don't have room for.

Bi-directional mainline railroading itself being somewhat of a challenge in a 5 x 9 (HO) area, the properties and possibilities of the dogbone, however extended, disguised, or folded, rate considerable discussion, pointing out that the first crossover puts you into a reversing-loop situation. Access questions that arise in even this small a plan when multiple levels of trackage are overlapped to gain route mileage must be addressed; a suggested circus-tent approach skips the annoyances of an access-hatch, while accommodating larger scales. Once the line is under the hills it can connect with as much layover trackage (we would now call it staging) as can be reached via accessible turnouts.

It's unfortunately still true that arranging aisleways to retain no-stoop access the full length of both the mainline and a branching branch is not just difficult—it's impossible, unless the junction is at an unlikely altitude above head height.

An Erie-Lackawanna wayfreight drops cars for
Dansville & Mt. Morris RR.

East Hill, rising some 700 feet in the next 11 miles and crossing the divide into the basin of the Susquehanna. At 1.3 per cent the line passes Dansville over 400 feet above the valley where the principal industry (a marine boiler plant) and the other traffic sources associated with a small town are located. So, here is our prototype for a "nonbranching" branchline, one which snuggles conveniently close to the line with which it connects, yet has a job to do in overcoming the vertical mismatch between its terminal and the main track.

SPRINGER & CINCINNATUS

The remaining segment of the Dansville & Mount Morris is freight only and operates a train only when there is some traffic. The palmier-day D&MM, when it also connected with its parent Erie at Mount Morris (six miles farther to the north than Groveland), is worthy of treatment in a larger layout which takes advantage of the added interest of connections with two larger roads. Therefore, for a minimum-space version of the basic idea we go theoretical and model the busier Springer & Cincinnatus. The S&C is 5 x 9 feet (in HO) for the basic reason that you can't quite fit this type of plan into the prevalent 4 x 8 space without losing too much of the contrasts between main and branch lines. As partial recompense, it can be built and operated (and is in fact more realistic) with one end butted against a wall.

The main line to which the S&C is tributary is represented well by the classic folded dogbone of the narrow-shank type (see fig. 1), which provides the illusion of point-to-point traffic on a double-track road. Incidentally, this is an ideal arrangement for use with the simplified block signal automatic train control outfits now becoming available; two trains can follow each other around the perimeter of the "bone" without either presenting an obvious nose-to-tail effect (it's almost a scale 1½ miles per lap) or requiring much attention on those occasions when you just feel like seeing them roll.

At Springer there's a mainline coaling station for the steam hogs and the beginning of a 2½ per cent grade extending up past Cincinnatus Station. Helpers can be used on the heavier drags, spending their time between trips in the tiny engine terminal, while downhill freights make use of the delay while the locomotive is being fueled to get the retainers turned down, releasing the brakes which were held applied as the train was eased into the valley. Occasionally, of course, cars destined for the branch are set out on the stub sidings at left and right.

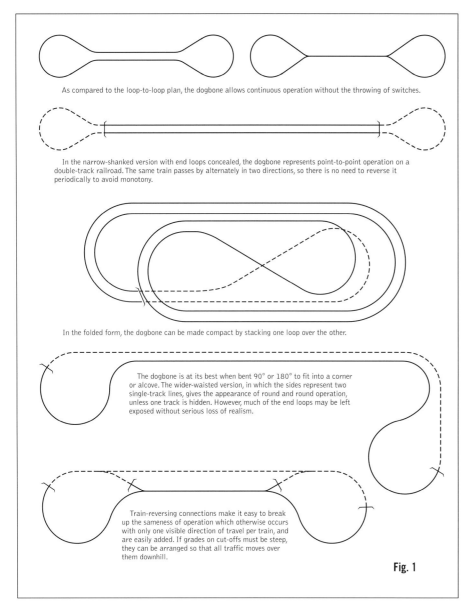

As compared to the loop-to-loop plan, the dogbone allows continuous operation without the throwing of switches.

In the narrow-shanked version with end loops concealed, the dogbone represents point-to-point operation on a double-track railroad. The same train passes by alternately in two directions, so there is no need to reverse it periodically to avoid monotony.

In the folded form, the dogbone can be made compact by stacking one loop over the other.

The dogbone is at its best when bent 90° or 180° to fit into a corner or alcove. The wider-waisted version, in which the sides represent two single-track lines, gives the appearance of round and round operation, unless one track is hidden. However, much of the end loops may be left exposed without serious loss of realism.

Train-reversing connections make it easy to break up the sameness of operation which otherwise occurs with only one visible direction of travel per train, and are easily added. If grades on cut-offs must be steep, they can be arranged so that all traffic moves over them downhill.

Fig. 1

While a tonnage train is toiling up the grade it's in the way of speedier traffic and most likely to be overtaken, so a facing-point crossover at Springer and a trailing-point crossover near the summit at Cincinnatus Station allow passing moves with a minimum of delay. Now, as fig. 2 shows, as soon as these crossovers are cut in we have a reversing-loop situation as far as two-rail wiring is concerned, and arrangements must be made for suitably changing the polarity of the sections between the crossovers in order to make this interesting and prototypically sincere maneuver. The end loops keep their basic polarities because there's no operating reason for running a train around them in the reverse direction should a hotshot which has passed a drag by taking the left-hand track up the hill stay on the wrong main after passing the Cincinnatus Station crossover, it's only the niceties of two-rail electric propulsion that convert the resulting impasse from a subterranean head-on collision into a mere short circuit.

It's well to leave some holes in the middle of the layout so that the concealed ends of the dogbone are accessible, and to provide as many hideaway tracks as are needed to accommodate your roster of equipment. The scenery can even take circus-tent form over the entire center of the layout and still leave good access from below while hiding the secrets of the plan from even the tallest onlooker.

The S&C line itself ambles past a few industries on the outskirts of Springer, past a site for a future spur at Brownsville, and into Cincinnatus, where there is a run-around track so that the various sidings serving the town's major factory can be switched conveniently and the train can make itself up in proper order for the return trip. An elevated conveyor between two buildings is shown, to tie the lower-level scene together and further emphasize its separateness from the main line up on the hillside above.

The turntable at Springer means only that the S&C's engine can occasionally change its heading and run forward from the junction to Cincinnatus instead of vice versa; there being no turning facilities at the other end of the branch, one wrong-way journey per trip is unavoidable. Likewise, mainline helpers must come back down the hill the way they went up, so you might consider the turntable just a concession to the feeling that no one should be without one of these most fascinating of railroad adjuncts, but that two would be a bit rich for a 5 x 9. The presence of the table is the cause of a feature that is the biggest nuisance of the track plan or its point of peak operating interest, depending on how you feel about a bit of adversity: All switching in the Springer yards, because there isn't enough width for a separate lead track, fouls one main track, while a run-around move ties 'em both up. It's not quite as bad as it might be—with both crossovers in reversed position a mainline train can scoot through while the switch crew is working either end of the little yard. The optional arrangement shown licks the problem, at the expense of a couple of spurs or the turntable, as you prefer.

The basic yard trackage of this plan may be revised slightly to be on a dead level so that construction can take the form of a platform with a simple ramp built up on it to carry the main line up the hill and support the upper loop. If you're building it as a bit more advanced job and want it to really have a soul, though, it will pay to go to the trouble of providing a depressed section for the little stream separating branch and main, and to build appropriate undulations into the grade of the S&C.

FRENCH BROAD VALLEY

A more expanded treatment of the same dogbone-and-branch scheme is the French Broad Valley plan, 10 x 18 feet in HO and fitting into a corner in basement or two-car garage. Most basement spaces would contain it in the larger gauges as well, but some redrawing of the trackage would be essential to avoid an excessive reach to the main

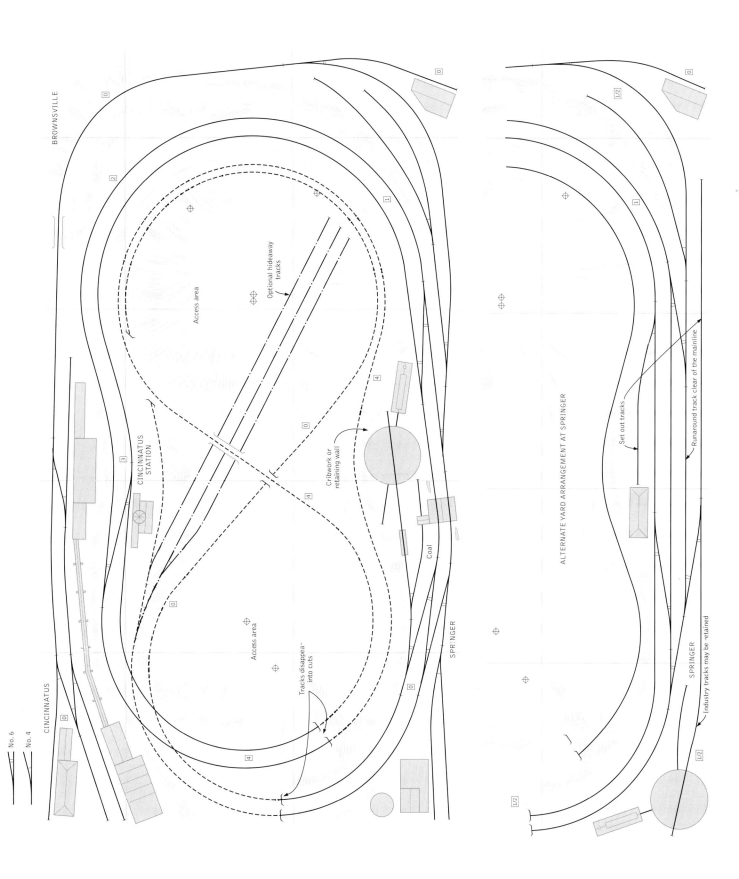

BROWNSVILLE

CINCINNATUS

No. 6
No. 4

CINCINNATUS STATION

Access area

Optional hideaway tracks

Cribwork or retaining wall

Access area

Tracks disappear into cuts

Coal

SPRINGER

ALTERNATE YARD ARRANGEMENT AT SPRINGER

Set out tracks

Runaround track clear of the mainline

Industry tracks may be retained

SPRINGER

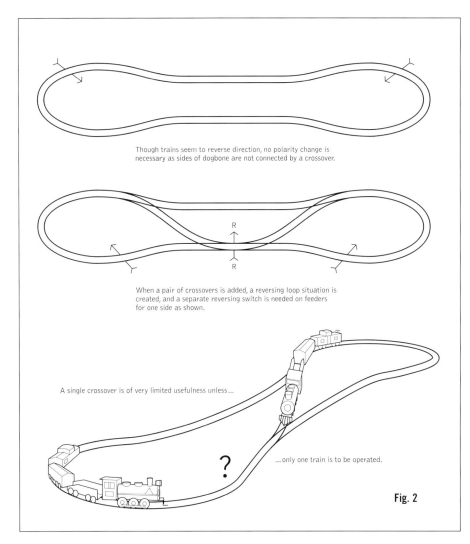

Though trains seem to reverse direction, no polarity change is necessary as sides of dogbone are not connected by a crossover.

When a pair of crossovers is added, a reversing loop situation is created, and a separate reversing switch is needed on feeders for one side as shown.

A single crossover is of very limited usefulness unless...

...only one train is to be operated.

Fig. 2

line, which in HO is already about at the limit of convenience.

The main line represents single track in this case, a fatter-waisted dogbone being used in nonfolded fashion, since there's more room and construction is simplified by not having stacked loops. From the upper yard limit of Lowassee a short but mean 3 per cent grade curves up to Digby and disappears quietly behind the mountain. The far side of the bone, generally hidden from view, brings the line back down at a more modest 1.6 per cent so that trains which are going downhill on the visible side of the loop won't need more than the road engine. The three passing tracks will each hold an 18 or 19 car train, so this road, though single track, is set up to handle a substantial tonnage in realistic style. Conventional-radius curves are used for the same purpose.

With this type of dogbone a train keeps going by in the same direction, so it's highly desirable to make it easy to

reverse traffic easily. The two cutoffs provided for this (A to B, C to D) are somewhat disguised in order to keep the plan from looking too much like an exercise in assembling tinplate segments into handy combinations. The C-D connection is made to look like an interchange track in Lowassee yard extending over to some other railroad, a logical need for freight coming off the branch line; the A-B connection is more of a sneak-off of the old school, creeping out of sight behind buildings and serving most of the time as a switching lead for the yard. It would be impossibly steep except that trains need only go over it downhill.

The Nether Digby branch starts out from Lowassee via a crazy mixed-up wye that is excused by the presumed desire to use the dam as a cheap way to get across the river. A steam plant taking up the load when the associated hydro power plant is caught with its water down is the first heavy-traffic plum on the line, closely followed by a pulp mill

getting some of its raw material via the river. At Moorefield there is a large what-have-you plant taking advantage of the plentiful water supply. The branch (which uses sharp-radius curves) horseshoes its way along the river, traverses a swamp on a wood trestle to pick up a little more atmosphere, recrosses the river and enters its terminal where an even half-dozen industry spurs justify using this long a branch to reach an area which obviously joins the main line up topside.

When the Nether Digby branch was a separate shortline company it naturally maintained its modest shops located at the end of the line from which the capital for building this connection to the main line had come. The larger road has continued to stable the engine working the branch in the two-stall house near the turntable, further justifying its existence by sending the helper engine working out of Lowassee over to Nether Digby for its monthly boiler wash. Thus do we contrive to keep the engine terminal out in front where it can be appreciated, while still emphasizing the branch which is the principal feature of the track plan.

Back at Lowassee the essential junction-point interchange yard is a sort of scraggly, single-ended affair. Otherwise, the turnouts would be too far from the edge of the layout for convenient construction and maintenance. As a result, the only run-around track is the main line passing siding. It's a long pull for a switcher making the trip around a short cut of cars, so the optional center crossover should be considered as a profitable improvement. There being another fairly bad grade from East End up to Lowassee, on very heavy trains a bit of big-time railroading flavor can be added by assigning one helper at East End and adding a second at the foot of the 3 per cent. What with the rugged grades on the branchline connections between Lowassee and East End and the industry tracks in that area, a husky switcher can spend the better part of the day shuffling things around town between trips to the top of the hill as the extra pusher.

We've got the prototype and it seems to work out rather nicely in the model, so if you want your heavy trains to have hills to climb and yet feel the need for some lower-pressure railroading of branchline spirit, consider the virtues of the nonbranching branch.

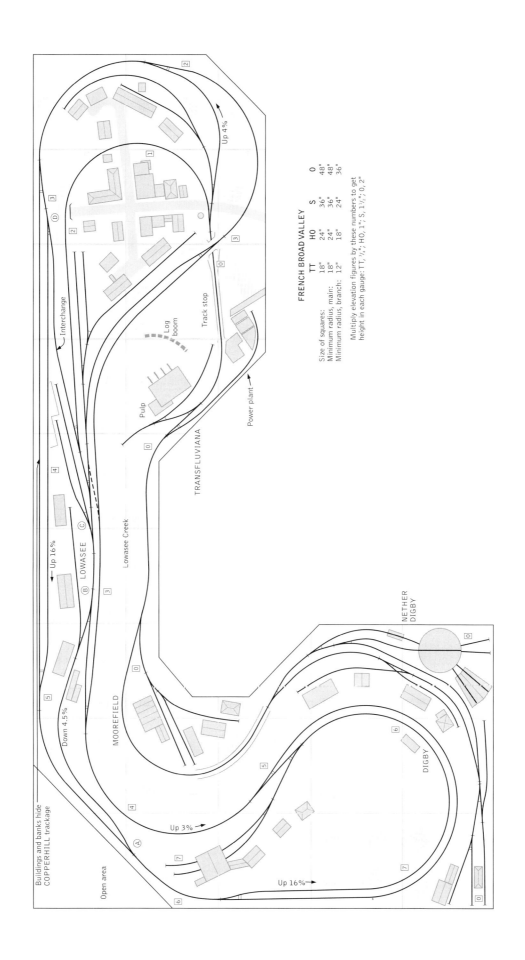

FRENCH BROAD VALLEY

	TT	HO	S	O
Size of squares:	18"	24"	36"	48"
Minimum radius, main:	18"	24"	36"	48"
Minimum radius, branch:	12"	18"	24"	36"

Multiply elevation figures by these numbers to get
height in each gauge: TT, ½"; HO, 1"; S, 1½"; O, 2"

Up 4%

Interchange

Track stop

Log boom

Pulp

Power plant

TRANSFLUVIANA

Up 16%

LOWASEE

Lowasee Creek

Down 4.5%

MOOREFIELD

Buildings and banks hide
COPPERHILL trackage

Open area

Up 3%

Up 16%

NETHER DIGBY

DIGBY

The Sociable Old Colony Lines

Here's a railroad designed strictly for operating

interest with a traffic flow that closely duplicates New Haven

operations in the Boston-Cape Cod area

MODEL RAILROADERS in general are a sociable lot and the traction fans seem to be even more so, if the popularity of trolley operating sessions in someone's home is any indication. Perhaps this is because of the ease of transporting a whole "train" or two of traction equipment, or perhaps the complicated operation that's possible and prototypical in this branch of the hobby is the major factor. Whatever the cause, there is no doubt that it's a happy situation for the sociably-inclined model rail to have a layout that offers interesting jobs for as many of the fraternity as may gather of an evening for some realistic railroading.

Steam-power devotees tend to favor the operation of long trains through less crowded and better-scenicked territory, but in keeping with the theme of fun and sociability through emphasis on railroadlike operation, here is a track plan that is a partial wedding of the operating interest of the traction line with the variety and relative modernity of the railroad. The prototype that lets us reconcile these opposites is the Old Colony portion of the New Haven, those lines running generally south and east from Boston. Old Colony's numerous commuter and short-distance passenger hauls and light freight traffic have been the despair of the railroad's treasury for many decades. Since even a decrepit model railroad runs trains at a rate to shade the actual traffic of a trunk line, and short trains are the factor that lets us put the essence of a whole division into a basement by the use of short sidings and terminal tracks, the New Haven's poison can be our meat.

As the map shows, the Old Colony (along with the associated trackage of the New Haven proper, such as the Boston-Providence portion of the main line) pretty well blankets eastern Massachusetts, even though many duplicating and interconnecting lines have been thinned out over the years.

Distances are short—it's only 120 miles from Boston all the way around the Cape to Provincetown—and the railroad is untypically like the typical model layout in that it has frequent junctions with itself.

New Englanders have been accustomed to commuting into the Hub by

Author's Insight

Unlike those on most track plan articles in the 1960 era, operations on the Old Colony feature relatively short trains, mostly passenger, running over a network of routes branching in catch-as-catch-can fashion throughout a fairly roomy and available but multi-purpose, already-subdivided basement with the usual complement of obstacles. The railroad's charter allows tracks to run anywhere except across the entrance at the foot of the stairs, so tentacles of line end in stubs or staging loops.

What the plan lacks in length of run it makes up in diversity of routes—just like this section of the New Haven; no fewer than nine junctions lead to nine points where runs terminate.

With the available control schemes of the article's era the Old Colony is a natural for multiple local panels, with the question of aisle width vs. operator girth moot since there are no aisles. With today's radio DCC cabs operating crew members will tend to act and feel more like engineers than towermen but get a similar feeling of satisfaction in running a 1956 schedule.

With passenger service gradually returning to Old Colony territory at the start of the new century, the plan, which is adaptable to scales up to O within basements of rambler proportions, has good possibilities for contemporary modeling.

train for over a hundred years, and copious schedules covering a somewhat extended "rush hour" have been necessary to soothe the Proper Bostonians who desire to get to town at a time befitting the social stature of their respective positions. The resulting losses from relatively short and frequent trains, together with the usual harsh tax situation on railroad property, have had the lines on the ropes for years.

As far back as the early '30s, the New Haven was chronically on the verge of eliminating all Old Colony passenger service. World War II came along, and later, the RDC. With the determination of some of the colorful company managements to seek financial improvement through service betterment, the trains were repeatedly reprieved. Finally, some direct subsidy from on-line communities kept the trains run-

ning for an extra year, starting in June, 1958. The sands ran out and the service is no more, but we need go back only to 1956 to find a relatively fat timetable to copy and we can legitimately squeeze the maximum of trackage interest into a minimum of space by using readily-available double-ended diesels and RDCs for our motive power.

As a sociable sort of line, our version of the Old Colony shares the fairly small basement (typical of that beneath a six-room, two-story house of modest proportions) with a fireplace-equipped recreation room. There's a laundry to contend with, as well as the inevitable furnace and water heater. However, as a pike featuring operational possibilities at the expense of scenic realism, it is free to wind its tentacles into any available nooks and crannies. At times, adjacent tracks, which are supposed to represent

No. 1335 steams eastbound with a passenger train, while a set of DL109s departs westbound with the *Senator* in tow.

lines that are miles apart, must snuggle close together.

In these cases, we do what we can to keep them scenically separate by using thin (virtually silhouette) representations of the rocky terrain, abundant foliage, and close-packed buildings so common in New England. The scheme in which the various main and branch lines hook together is the thing that lets this plan represent the prototype operation, so major twisting in the trackage to fit any particular space situation is possible without damaging the basic idea.

The track plan is shown in HO scale in a 22 x 28-foot basement, with 24" radius curves to permit handling full-length passenger equipment over all

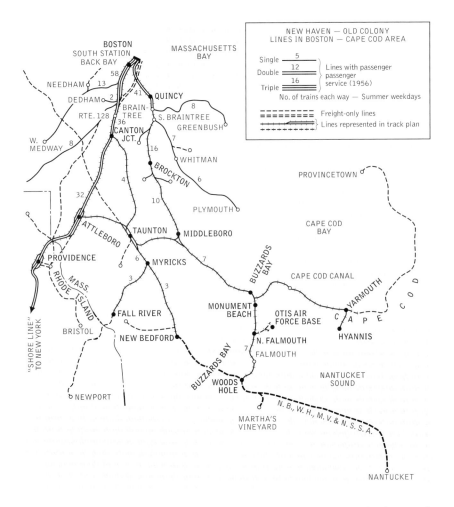

NEW HAVEN — OLD COLONY
LINES IN BOSTON — CAPE COD AREA

Single ————5————
Double ══════12══════ } Lines with passenger passenger service (1956)
Triple ═══════16═══════

No. of trains each way — Summer weekdays

– – – – – – – – Freight-only lines
╫╫╫╫╫╫╫╫ Lines represented in track plan

lines. In a one-story house of equivalent size, the same scheme can be worked out in S or O gauge. It's fairly big as layouts go, perhaps too big for the average model railroader to build and maintain singlehanded, but quite appropriate for the man who has a fellow rail, or two or three, working with him. It will take several people to operate the beast to advantage anyway, so this is just as well. Finally, it's a natural for building and putting into operation in easy stages, since the various branches can be built one at a time, each addition increasing the fun and providing continuing incentive to keep up work sessions.

As the map indicates, we have left out many of the New Haven's lines in the area, but still have a pretty fancy knot of trackage left, with no fewer than nine junctions and the same number of passenger train destinations represented.

TRACK PLAN ANGLES

We can start our inspection tour from Providence by emerging from the hidden loop in the lower left corner. This is in the low-rent (furnace room) district, and if space is available, the number of holdover tracks could well

be increased to handle the heavy Shore Line traffic for which the New Haven is noted. As in the prototype, our line to Boston is multiple-track, with the two through tracks being supplemented by a third through Attleboro and for the last stretch into Boston's South Station. In this densely populated territory, there are industry sidings at close intervals all the way, but these are carefully planned as trailing-point spurs for right-hand traffic, because the traffic would make the extra maneuvers needed to switch "wrong way" sidings too much of a burden.

We don't have room to represent Route 128 Station, the oddly-named postwar stop that the New Haven instituted to serve the belt highway along which a major part of the booming missile electronic industry is located; however, we do have a condensation of Back Bay Station since it is actually right over the tracks and so we get some additional operating interest free.

South Station is a stub terminal which we condense to four tracks; we can do without that half of its trackage which serves the Boston and Albany, but again, if space permits, we could

well add another pair of platform tracks. A double slip switch will increase flexibility of train routing through the throat, and this is at least as accessible a place as you could ask for one of the little gems.

To inspect the Fall River-New Bedford line, we will start out by retracing the main line to Canton Junction, where a slight curve to the left leads into the single-track line to Taunton. The layout has been confined to a narrow shelf along the wall of the recreation room at most points, so this junction can't have the sharp curve of the prototype and we will use a "flat" of a factory to make it clear that we're taking off in a different direction. This would be a good place to steal another few inches of width if you can get away with it. A TV set built into the layout might help.

At the junction we notice that the New Haven uses both right-hand and left-hand semaphore signals indiscriminately. As a hedge against the possibility of extension of the mainline electrification from New Haven to Boston, the paddles on the through tracks were made to extend to the left, for the most part, so that future catenary-supporting bridges wouldn't obscure them from the right-hand side of the cab.

We pass through Taunton on a short stretch of double track and then keep to the right on single track to Myricks, where the New Bedford and Fall River branches diverge. Our Fall River terminus has a runaround track and several industrial spurs; the main track gains a precious few inches of length by diving under another part of the layout, ostensibly en route to the Ferry St. station where the old Fall River Line steamers to New York used to connect with the boat train from Boston. Our New Bedford line is much more condensed and merely crawls behind some scenery and dies as a double stub. With our double-ended motive power, however, it still can provide for reasonably genuine-looking traffic on its approaches.

A trip back to Boston prepares us for inspection of the most highly-developed part of the track plan, the Cape Cod lines. The main track for these points leaves the Providence-New York line right at the station throat. The dense-traffic section of the line to Braintree, which in prototype also carries trains to Greenbush and Plymouth, is represented here by a second track extending as far as Quincy Adams. This track also serves as the runaround track for the stub tracks in South Station—we can't afford to use space for single-purpose trackage around this pike!

Brockton's passing track allows us to use it as a terminating point for some midday local runs into Boston, as in the real Old Colony operating scheme, and this portion of the line is somewhat higher than the Providence line so we can see what's going on at the back of the shelf. Then our Cape Cod main stem drops rapidly to stay out of the way of other tracks that must also get through the doorway by the fireplace.

Some of the grades on this pike are fairly severe, since they are required to let us stack tracks above each other where space is tight. The actual Old Colony territory is rugged and rocky, but grades are short, as in our case, and do not constitute much of a problem for train operation. With the short trains we can handle, the same thing applies in the model. The principal consideration is to avoid having sharply-graded tracks out

in the open where they might make the railroad look like a roller coaster.

Our line emerges again at Middle-boro, another terminus for commuter trains. Then comes Buzzard Bay, a neat white station on a curve which is the real hot spot of the railroad.

Next comes the best scenic opportunity on the road, the vertical-lift bridge across the Cape Cod canal which, until recently (when it was shaded a few feet by the B&O's new Arthur Kill bridge to Staten Island), was the longest of its type in the world. In true scale, its 544-foot span would work out at about 6 feet in HO, but a condensed version can still be impressive and also helpful in avoiding a bottleneck if you make it an operating model; naturally, a principal consideration in the planning of the whole pike was to locate this feature where it would do the most good access-wise. Incidentally, the Oct. '55 *Trains* has a well-illustrated feature on this bridge.

The switch marking the parting of the ways for the Hyannis and Woods Hole lines is right on the eastern approach span of the canal bridge. Our Hyannis line is not very scenic because it winds up in the laundry, but it provides a spur to represent a source and destination of carloads from or for the freight-only Provincetown branch, an intermediate passing track, and essential run-around facilities at its terminal.

The Woods Hole line winds up on the mantel and bookshelves in the rec

OLD COLONY LINES

Scale of drawing: ¼" = 1'-0"

	HO	S	O
Min. radius (main line)	24"	36"	48"

Multiply elevation figures by the following to determine height for each scale: HO, 1"; S, 1½"; O, 2".

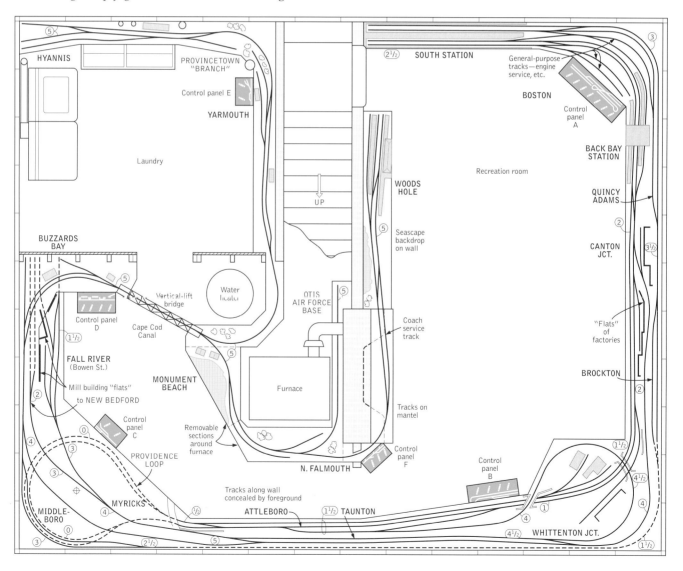

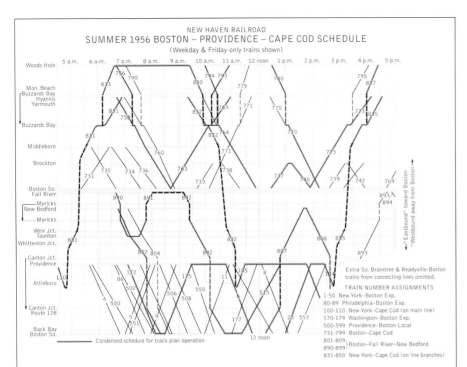

TRAIN NUMBER ASSIGNMENTS

1-50 New York–Boston Exp.
80-89 Philadelphia–Boston Exp.
100-110 New York–Cape Cod (on main line)
170-179 Washington–Boston Exp.
500-599 Providence–Boston Local
731-799 Boston–Cape Cod
801-809 Boston–Fall River–New Bedford
890-899
831-850 New York–Cape Cod (on line branches)

Extra So. Braintree & Readyville-Boston
trains from connecting lines omitted.

Condensed schedule for track plan operation

room, after some moderately harrowing experiences getting around the furnace. To avoid comment from the fire marshal, the segments close to the furnace may have to be removable between operating sessions, but this should be no great problem. A substandard radius spur leads into Otis Air Force Base and provides one of the major reasons for freight business on the line. The Woods Hole terminal is, for once, an essentially noncondensed version of the very compact prototype. Every turnout is duplicated and the actual capacity of the tracks is only slightly greater than provided here.

THE *CAPE CODDER* ROUTE

The rest of the trackage in the plan is devoted to representing the most interesting route in the system, the line followed by the summer-only *Cape Codder* trains from New York. Retracing our route from Hyannis or Woods Hole past Buzzards Bay, we turn off the Boston line just south of Middleboro and cut over to the Boston-Fall River-New Bedford line just south of Taunton. We follow the double track to Whittenton Junction, where we swing wide to the left and join the Boston-Providence line at Attleboro, but now we are headed away from Boston. That makes us a westbound train on the time card; since its lines are more or less radially arranged, New Haven keeps things straight by defining trains headed toward Boston as eastbound and vice versa.

Cramped space means that our Taunton-Attleboro line must cross over the main line a couple of times, but otherwise we are able to work in an essentially correct representation of all this interweaving. This same kind of flitting from one line to another through reversing loops occurs in most typical "bowl of spaghetti" track plans, but it's nice for once to have a prototype for it.

When it comes to operating this many-armed monster, we can settle a few things quickly. In the first place, it's always summertime on the Old Colony. Since Cape Cod traffic is primarily of resort nature, the summer schedule is much heavier and more varied. Furthermore, we might as well plan to represent Fridays and Sundays most of the time, since half the name trains on this part of the railroad operate on a once-weekly basis. With these ground rules, we have no need to go beyond the truth when it comes to setting up a busy schedule with numerous points of intense operating interest. Take a look at the schedule graph for the lines we represent, based upon the summer timetable for 1956.

Some of the subtleties of the operation become apparent only after considerable study, but several of the ways in which the New Haven was already operating, in a manner as interesting as anything a railfan could dream up, can be seen readily.

For example, look at the classic pattern of commuter traffic on the Boston-Cape Cod line at the top. There's a morning inbound rush, with trains originating from two distances from the terminal (Middleboro and Woods Hole-Hyannis) no. 758 makes all the stops from Middleboro to Boston; no. 760, following, runs express from Middleboro to give the folks from the Cape a shorter trip and is scheduled so that it almost catches up by the time South Station is reached. During the middle of the day, traffic is lighter. There are the family trains to and from the Cape, while supplementary service to closer points is provided by shuttle trains between South Station and Brockton, the largest city on the line. There is not enough traffic from the stations between Brockton and Middleboro to warrant starting these runs at the more distant terminal as is done during the morning rush hour.

BUZZARDS BAY BUSINESS

As the many interconnecting lines on the schedule indicate, Buzzards Bay is one of the busiest places on the railroad. Every train to or from the Cape terminals splits or is consolidated at this point, except for one case (not shown) in which passengers from Woods Hole change trains there. When eastbound and westbound trains meet at Buzzards Bay, this means four trains are involved. When an additional pair of trains is nearby, as is the case around 10 a.m., the importance of making meets at places like Monument Beach instead of Buzzards Bay becomes critical (there are only two platform tracks at the junction station), and the dispatcher can keep busy even without the help of such complications as extra cars on week ends, baggage-handling delays, and the like.

The actual process of combining the trains offers considerable variety too. Some trains such as 790-760 are made up of regular commuter coaches hauled by road-switchers, which are rearranged and then operated in multiple for the rest of the trip to South Station.

The *Day Cape Codder*, operating daily from mid-June to mid-September, starts from Woods Hole as a three-car, road-switcher-powered streamliner. Its baggage-parlor car is trailed by two coaches. Many of the patrons have made a ten-minute connection from the *SS Nantucket* of the state-owned New Bedford, Woods Hole, Martha's Vineyard & Nantucket Steamship Authority.

Running as no. 830, our *Codder* fills its remaining seats at six stops in the 17 miles to Buzzards Bay. The normally open lift bridge over the canal remains

A pair of DL109s, with the New York-Cape Cod *Cape Codder* in tow, threads through the longest vertical lift bridge in the world, which spans the Cape Cod Canal at Buzzards Bay, Massachusetts.

down after 830's passage, for no. 832, the Hyannis section, with a full-length grill car, two coaches, and a parlor-baggage car in that order behind its road passenger diesel, is hard on its heels. Combining these two consists is a straightforward process, and the Hyannis engine soon takes off for Grand Central Station with the resulting seven-car, baggage-at-each-end train.

But before it can leave the station, no. 763, an RDC consist from Boston, must arrive and clear the single track. Separating the Budd-car train into Hyannis and Woods Hole sections is simplicity itself, and the cars for the 23.5-mile trip to Hyannis leave promptly under their own power. The road-switcher which brought the *Day Cape Codder* up from Woods Hole needs to go back for a midday stint in local freight service, though, so it couples up to the two passenger cars and hauls them, their motors idling, down the shore of Buzzards Bay as train no. 793. This saves one engine crew and means that the Boston-bound RDC running as no. 794 can get past the whole outfit at once at Monument Beach. Since 794 has to back into the single-ended passing track, this is a great help.

Weekends call for real maneuvering on the limited trackage on the Cape. The Friday-only *Night Cape Codder* with as many as six Pullmans out of Grand Central, plus an additional Washington sleeper picked up from the *Bar Harbor* at New Haven, takes the intricate *Cape Codder* route via Attleboro, Taunton and Middleboro and pulls into Buzzards Bay at 6 a.m., running due east by the compass but westbound as no. 831 by the timetable. Two extra Friday-evening-only trains have already come into Hyannis and Woods Hole. The *Sand Dune* brings weekending husbands from Boston to their families spending the summer on the Cape, and the *Neptune* carries coach and parlor car passengers from New York after the close of business.

There is no space at the terminals for all this equipment to await its Sunday evening return to the cities, so it must be deadheaded back out of the way before the *Night Codder* can head for its twin destinations and park its Pullmans. To minimize this non-revenue movement, of course, the trackage at the terminals is kept full—a good chance for some interesting planning on your part in your trainmaster role.

The New Bedford-Fall River route is a somewhat simpler operation, with RDC equipment for most runs. Note how no. 890 provides a connection at Taunton and then returns to Fall River as no. 891, to prepare for a through run to Boston. It leaves Taunton just in time to meet no. 804 while still on the double track just outside of town. Freight traffic is heavier than on the Cape, though, so our trackage is well used.

The Shore Line route of the New Haven, which we represent from Boston to Providence, can be as busy as you want. As an out-and-back proposition with a fairly short run, it would be difficult to keep supplied with trains except that most consists, whether headed for New York, Philadelphia, or Washington, are not turned at South Station but merely provided with a fresh locomotive (double-ended) at the stern and sent westward.

To duplicate the rush hour traffic shown on the schedule for all our lines would take about twelve sets of equipment, more than the trackage would accommodate. I've therefore indicated a reduced schedule (in color) which gives the flavor of the traffic on all lines, with about half as many trains. Actually, if two or three men are operating the railroad, it can best be done by operating the Cape Cod, Fall River-New Bedford and Boston-Providence lines intensively but individually, in sequence, with the interline *Cape Codders* to tie all the episodes together.

WIRING

For my money, there's not much point in running trains if you can't see them, at least at the more interesting parts of their runs where switching, meeting, and passing other trains are involved. So, any single control panel for this octopus can't possibly do the job. At the six locations shown on the track plan, there are panels of varying completeness. Seven cabs with individual power supplies are provided. However, each cab can be operated over some of its routes from more than one panel, so its operator can move around and be present at the scene of action most of the time.

It's still a real challenge to run in smart New England style, so despite the location in the rec room, you'd better enforce Rule G until after the *Owl* has headed into the night with its snoozing New Yorkers, winding up a happy time with good companions and a pike that's planned and scheduled for the most in operating fun.

To Hardscrabble the Hard Way

Action-packed narrow gauge branch tailored for

HOn3 can also be built in O, HO, or other scales

THERE WAS a time when you could ride 3-foot gauge Denver & Rio Grande track all the way across the Rockies to Grand Junction and beyond. Nevertheless, when thinking of narrow gauge American railroading, we are likely to recall only decrepit branches with twice- or thrice-a-week mixed trains rattling over weed-covered right of way.

Branches and short lines make fine models, but suppose your primary interest is in running and watching lots of trains—interweaving stock extras, ore drags, and parlor-car-equipped passenger runs on a single-track mountain railroad—operating in the way made vivid by Gil Lathrop's stories of busy days on the big hill. Let's see what can be done to catch the spirit of a narrow gauge line that really moves traffic.

Our space is an 11 x 12-foot basement alcove. We'll model a 3-foot gauge prototype. In HO this makes the track gauge .413″ or HOn3.

We have access along most of the open side, a space quite free from obstructions, and there are no low windows. The hitch is that the area must also house a king-size rolltop desk which is to serve as a worktable and hold an extensive railroad library and a lantern collection. In common with all major American narrow gauge lines, our road must have access to the rest of the country by way of an affiliated standard gauge connection.

For our heavy-traffic, dispatcher's delight pike, a point-to-point main line which has quick-turnaround provisions at each end is the ideal, so we must try to work in either a loop or a wye at both terminals.

Since narrow gauge trackage is usually a sightly and mostly handcrafted affair, we will try to devise some reasonable, prototypical basis for leaving most of these turnaround tracks and turnouts exposed to view.

As it is an impossible assignment to provide enough visible traffic sources to keep even 25-ton cars loaded in the volume we require, an imaginary portion of our line must wander on into the mines and forests of the hinterland. On the other hand, we can revel in the freedom of using the steep (4 per cent or even more) grades and sharp (18″ radius) curves which are so characteristic of railroads that are built narrow because they must penetrate rough country cheaply.

Author's Insight

Operationally and scenically, *concentrated* railroading is the name of the game for the Pueblo & Salt Lake. The assignment is to fit a paraphrase of the standard gauge main line and a connecting narrow gauge branch of the Denver & Rio Grande into a space that, adjusting for the fact that it must be entered from the side and accommodate such interlopers as a roll-top desk/workbench, equates to only 20 HO or 35 HOn3 square squares.

A bent dogbone with only one side of its shank exposed takes care of the essential standard gauge presence in a walk-in, walkaround plan, but coming up with a plausible, fairly heavy-traffic point-to-point narrow gauge main with significant out-of-sight but accessible staging takes every trick in the book, some of them rather innovative at the time:

• An exposed turnaround loop at the dual-gauge junction end.
• Lengthy side-by-side trackage, justified by a horseshoe curve (which just happens to contain a wye for turning helpers).
•Extensive second-deck section, high enough for reasonable lower-deck scenic treatment.
• Wye junction termination of the modeled line, with tails providing hidden train-length turnaround capability and multi-train out-of-sight but fully accessible staging.

THE MCLEOD VALLEY BOOM

Our search for prototype justification for our railroad goes something like this. As shown in fig. 1, the main line of the standard gauge Pueblo & Salt Lake traverses this section of the mountains on a fairly easy, water-grade alignment along the Lewis River. In the mid-1880s, a somewhat pessimistic prospector struck it rich at a point on the McLeod River, a point which he promptly named Hardscrabble. The P&SL began surveys for a branch, probably standard gauge, up the McLeod from Jahvis. This would afford an easy but roundabout route for ore concentrates from the new mining area to the smelters which were already in business in Smelter City at the mouth of Coal Creek. (From here a branch reaches the fuel deposits up Coal Creek.) Before construction started, however, a bunch of optimists hit pay dirt in the course of an expedition downstream from Triple Divide Pass and equally promptly dubbed the watercourse Bonanza Creek and the place Golconda.

With timber and ranching possibilities in the new country, this second rich strike tipped the scales. The P&SL management now reconsidered the findings of its surveyors and laid out a new route through the previously unimportant Wind Gap in the Mule Shoe Mountains, Cameo Canyon, and the Triple Divide country. This line, saving a couple of hundred miles en route to the smelter, could serve both old and new mining areas, but the wicked curvature of the canyons to be traversed multiplied the

Denver & Rio Grande dual-gauge (standard and 3-foot gauge) trackage in Alamosa, Colorado.

number of tunnels required for a practical standard gauge alignment. Thus was born the 3-foot gauge McLeod River Division of the parent road.

A closer look at three key areas shows how nature was kind to the model railroader in the convolutions forced upon the locating engineers as they did their best with the harsh topography they were called upon to penetrate. Wind Gap was a prehistoric route of the Lewis River before a slide or earthquake caused its diversion to its present course. This opening in the mountain range was the logical point of divergence from the main line, but its altitude and the narrowness of the

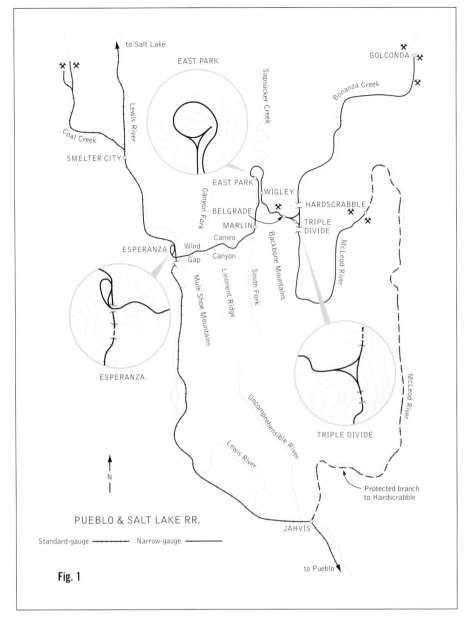

to Salt Lake

GOLCONDA

EAST PARK

Sapsucker Creek

Bonanza Creek

Lewis River

Coal Creek

SMELTER CITY

EAST PARK

WIGLEY

HARDSCRABBLE

Canyon Fork

BELGRADE

MARLIN

TRIPLE DIVIDE

McLeod River

Cameo

ESPERANZA

Wind

Gap

Canyon

Backbone Mountains

Mule Shoe Mountains

Liniment Ridge

South Fork

McLeod River

ESPERANZA

Uncomprehensible River

TRIPLE DIVIDE

N

Lewis River

Protected branch
to Hardscrabble

PUEBLO & SALT LAKE RR.

Standard-gauge ┼┼┼┼┼┼   Narrow-gauge ────────

JAHVIS

to Pueblo

Fig. 1

canyon at the logical junction site, Esperanza, resulted in a route requiring a short stretch of 8 per cent grade. This was too much, even though it would only be against the direction of travel of empty cars. The valley was wide enough, however, to permit a flying junction arrangement with a sort of spiral connection at a more practical 2 per cent grade. Thus a turning loop for one end of our HOn3 line miraculously came into being.

Cameo Canyon is crooked but level and leads nicely into the valley of Sapsucker Creek. For the first few miles downstream, though, the gorge is so narrow that a mountain goat would have to be articulated to be able to turn himself around. So the branch line continues on downstream to East Park simply because there is nothing else it can

do. A lot of altitude is going to have to be gained before the summit at Triple Divide Pass will be surmounted, and the normal procedure would be to maintain a steady grade from Marlin on to the top. Because this would require a rather expensive high-level crossing of the creek at East Park, the P&SL elected to stay near the water level until after the loopback, accepting the resulting 4 per cent climb from there to the pass. The decision to save construction costs at the expense of operating problems later gives us a chance to use helper engines and have a good long main line without getting too close to the basement ceiling.

ENDING IT ALL

At Triple Divide the locating engineers, who had followed instructions to

the letter so far and gotten by without a tunnel,* ran out of luck. Two short bores are essential to let the divided line enter the Bonanza Creek and McLeod River valleys, but the arrangement just happens to be such that in our 3.5 mm. reproduction we will be able to use a wye to terminate the portion of the railroad we model in the flesh. The imaginary remaining trackage takes the steam cars to Golconda and Hardscrabble on a generally easy downward gradient through broadening valleys which, once the mining fever has subsided a bit, will provide many tons of pinto beans, peaches, cattle, and forest products to diversify our consists.

Translating the McLeod River Division into a practical pike plan involves a little unconventional but not particularly risky construction. The Esperanza yards, located against the masonry outer wall, fig. 2, are on solid construction, remarkable only because bookcases of neat but not elegant construction support the tabletop and most of the space beneath the railroad is put to use. Slightly smaller volumes will have to be selected for the shelf under the turntable pit, but since switches are controlled by manual stands there is relatively little under-the-table wiring and the poorer-than-average access is not a problem.

The remainder of the standard gauge trackage consists of a level, concealed dogbone of 22″ minimum radius (44″ for O scale, etc.) suitable for operating equipment appropriate for whatever era you may choose. Two crossovers, hidden but quite accessible, fig. 2, allow interchanging and reversing the mainline trains; additional layover trackage can be added if desired.

Operating the Esperanza yards is a game in itself. Inbound narrow gauge passenger and mixed trains pop out of Wind Gap, cross over the main line and the river on a slightly shaky trestle, and literally fall into town by way of the 8 per cent cutoff behind the station. A backing move spots the passenger cars by the station, leaving the engine free to shove the freight cars into the transshipment shed track. There is no narrow gauge runaround track in the yard,

---

* Frequent tunnels are not characteristic of the general minimum-cost approach of American narrow gauge. On the entire D&RGW narrow gauge network there were, and are, only two tunnels, both short.

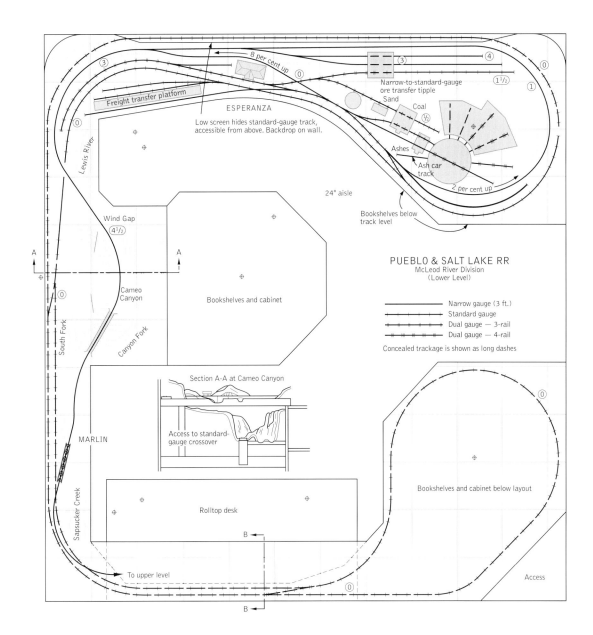

Fig. 2

[Figure labels, reading within the diagram:]

8 per cent up

Narrow-to-standard-gauge ore transfer tipple

Sand

Coal

Ashes

Ash car track

2 per cent up

Freight transfer platform

ESPERANZA

Low screen hides standard-gauge track, accessible from above. Backdrop on wall.

Lewis River

24" aisle

Bookshelves below track level

Wind Gap

4½

A   A

Cameo Canyon

Canyon Fork

South Fork

Bookshelves and cabinet

PUEBLO & SALT LAKE RR
McLeod River Division
(Lower Level)

Narrow gauge (3 ft.)	
Standard gauge	
Dual gauge — 3-rail	
Dual gauge — 4-rail	

Concealed trackage is shown as long dashes

Section A-A at Cameo Canyon

Access to standard-gauge crossover

MARLIN

Sapsucker Creek

Rolltop desk

Bookshelves and cabinet below layout

B   B

To upper level

Access

---

so all McLeod Valley trains head for the hills via the loop track's more modest grade, whether or not their power could overcome 8 per cent with the tonnage at hand.

Ore trains coming into Esperanza must follow a different procedure. The locomotive leaves its loads standing on the main line, cuts off, and retreats down the cutoff. The brakemen then let the cars roll down into the upper-level ore tipple tracks, where their contents will be speedily transferred to standard gauge gondolas for the trip to the smelter. The caboose is dropped down the 8 per cent onto the incline, and all is ready for the return, with or without an extended visit to the engine service facilities, as the occasion may demand. Empties from the tipple yard are picked up from the upper level on the out-

bound trip, completing their turnaround without ever descending to the main yard level.

The fun comes when a few too many cars accumulate in Esperanza and some must be stashed away in the spur between the narrow- and standard gauge main lines, next to the roundhouse. This track faces the wrong way and so must be switched using the 8 per cent as a lead track. Hauling a few empties up the cutoff will really test the mettle of your little mills.

DUAL-GAUGE TRACKAGE

Figure 4 shows the arrangement of dual-gauge trackage in the Esperanza yard. In prototype and model, dual-gauge turnouts are intriguing affairs that come in no less than eight different versions and involve lots of extra frogs

and guard rails. Charles Small wrote all about them, including explanation of gapping, etc., in the July 1952 issue of *Model Railroder*. I have used the same letters Charlie used in classifying these turnouts at Esperanza. As would be the case in a real interchange yard, this one has been laid out to accomplish its functions with the minimum of special trackwork. Building dual-gauge turnouts is fun, and this yard uses the same type of turnout twice in only two cases.

In this particular yard, it is quite desirable to locate the third running rail on the side indicated in fig. 4. Having the narrow and standard gauge share the nearer rail would mean building six extra frogs and their accompanying guard rails. You can't very well have a locomotive's weight sitting eccentrically on a turntable, so a dual-gauge turntable

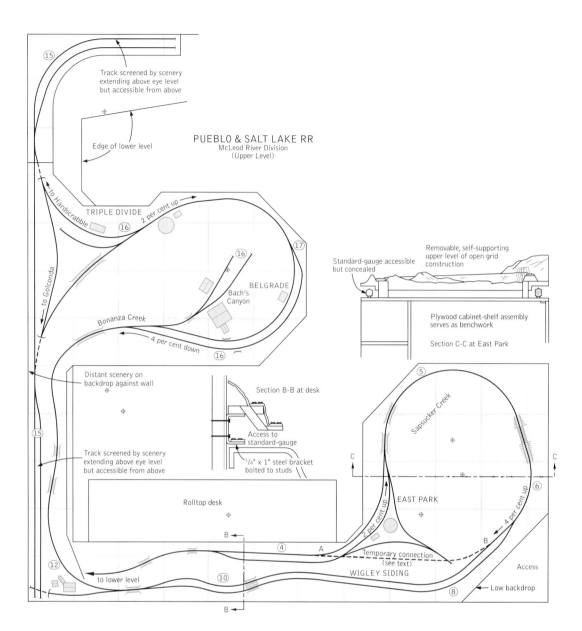

Fig. 3

(Labels within the figure:)

⑮

Track screened by scenery extending above eye level but accessible from above

Edge of lower level

PUEBLO & SALT LAKE RR
McLeod River Division
(Upper Level)

to Hardscrabble

TRIPLE DIVIDE

2 per cent up

⑯

⑰

⑯

BELGRADE

Bach's Canyon

to Golconda

Bonanza Creek

4 per cent down

⑯

Removable, self-supporting upper level of open grid construction

Standard-gauge accessible but concealed

Plywood cabinet-shelf assembly serves as benchwork

Section C-C at East Park

Distant scenery on backdrop against wall

Section B-B at desk

Access to standard-gauge

¼" x 1" steel bracket bolted to studs

Track screened by scenery extending above eye level but accessible from above

⑮

Rolltop desk

⑤

Sapsucker Creek

C

C

2 per cent up

EAST PARK

4 per cent up

⑥

B

B

Temporary connection (see text)

WIGLEY SIDING

Access

④

A

⑫

to lower level

⑩

⑧

Low backdrop

B

B

---

and any dual-gauge tracks in the enginehouse must have four rails. Separate leads are shown to bring the big and small engines to the table. This is the easy and unspectacular way to do it. For just a little more work, you can work in a rare but simple transition section and provide a nice conversation piece, fig. 5.

Dual-gauge operations at Esperanza are dictated by the nature of the traffic. Locomotive coal is received in standard gauge cars from the Coal Creek area, so the track by the coal dock is standard gauge; cinders are needed along the branch, so the ash car track matches the 3-foot cars only. The regular switcher at Esperanza is narrow gauge and handles the wide cars by use of an idler flat with appropriate coupler combinations at its two ends. Between times, this car is spotted on the spur by the station. The fact

that some mainline trains now terminate at Esperanza accounts for the dual-gauge engine servicing facilities; as it stands, the mainline crews must also switch the boxcars in and out of the tracks at the trans-shipment shed. A logical later step in development of the yard's flexibility would be dual-gauging the main line between yard limits, providing a runaround capability for the slim gauge boys at a cost of some six additional frogs and three more switchpoints.

ON THE ROAD

In any case, Esperanza can provide trains for the narrow gauge main line as fast as you need them, putting on a show typical of the heyday of mountain railroading.

As the cross sections of the layout in fig. 2 show, much of our main line is

supported by open-grid framework bracketed from the partition walls. After the first summit at Wind Gap—conquered with the aid of the Esperanza switcher shoving on the markers end, if necessary—the trend is gently downgrade through Cameo Canyon. Scenicking at this point is in the nature of a peek-through diorama, since there is another track platform far above the canyon-floor trackage. Its lower side is neatly enclosed and painted to represent the sky above the canyon scene, as shown in fig. 6. Curvature of the canyon walls is such that you cannot actually see all the way through, but the depth of the scene makes for an unusual degree of realism as the little train winds out of sight.

The train passes through Marlin beyond Cameo Canyon, lower left of

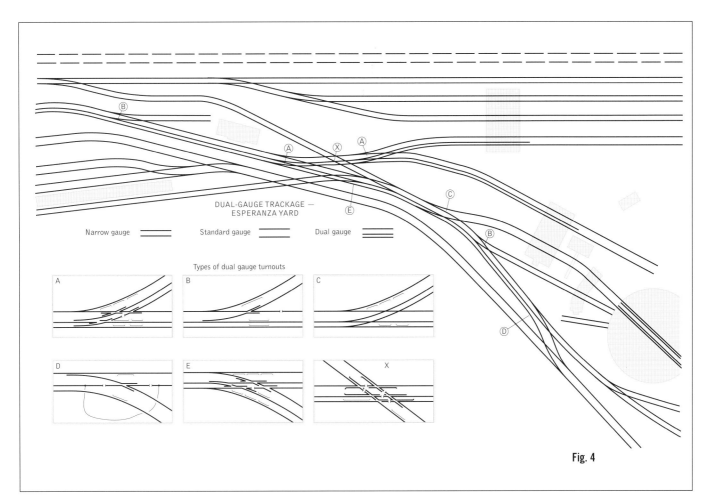

DUAL-GAUGE TRACKAGE —
ESPERANZA YARD

Narrow gauge ═══ Standard gauge ═══ Dual gauge ═══

Types of dual gauge turnouts

A   B   C

D   E   X

Fig. 4

fig. 2, and then turns with the bend in Sapsucker Creek. From here you see it at the words "To lower level" at the lower left of fig. 3. We are moving into upper-level territories now.

Entering East Park there's a standard-length passing track, matching our usual eight-car freight consists, and a wye on which there will usually be found a helper engine turned and ready for the hill. The 4 per cent starts just beyond the second crossing at Sapsucker as we head back upstream on a ledge cut in the hill side above the track we have so recently traversed. Wigley Siding is a double-length affair which is put to good use when ore production is heavy and solid trains of empties are dispatched to the mines. These drags rate doubleheaded power all the way, as well as a pusher out of East Park, and are scheduled to make meets only here where they can get by without having to stop in the middle of that boiler-busting climb.

Beyond Wigley our upper track, rounding the corner of the room, is rather subtly removed scenically from its relationship to the lower-level track and finds itself on a separate second-

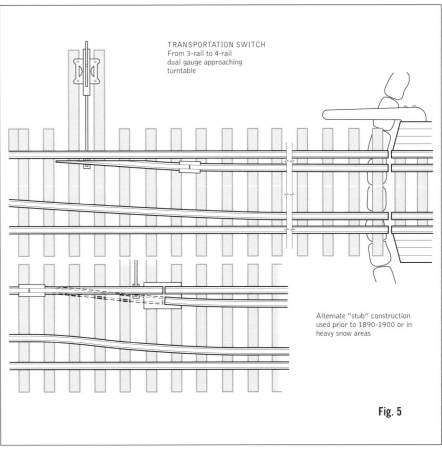

TRANSPORTATION SWITCH
From 3-rail to 4-rail dual gauge approaching turntable

Alternate "stub" construction used prior to 1890-1900 or in heavy snow areas

Fig. 5

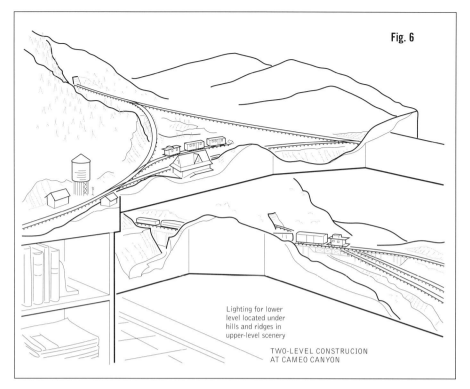

Fig. 6

Lighting for lower
level located under
hills and ridges in
upper-level scenery

TWO-LEVEL CONSTRUCION
AT CAMEO CANYON

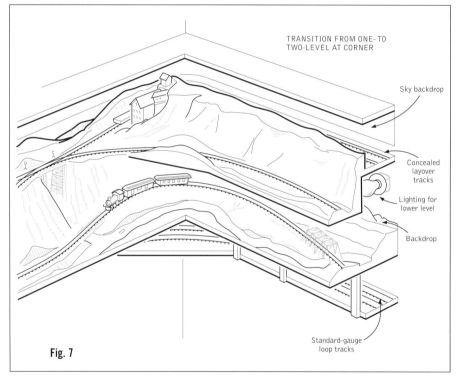

TRANSITION FROM ONE- TO
TWO-LEVEL AT CORNER

Sky backdrop

Concealed
layover
tracks

Lighting for
lower level

Backdrop

Standard-gauge
loop tracks

Fig. 7

level shelf, fig. 7 at right, on which it will proceed for the rest of its visible journey.

Switching the Bach's Canyon mine presents realistic problems. The cost of coal* in this remote area is such that it is highly desirable to leave empties here on

the way up rather than to take them to the top of the hill and bring them back, but this means considerable shuffling of cars on a grade where even poorly lubricated HOn3 rolling stock, left to itself for a moment without set brakes, will become runaway. You will probably settle for the use of chocks wedged between the ties in lieu of working handbrakes on most of your cars, but in any case it will keep you alert.

* Coal from Coal Creek mines has to go first to Smelter City, fig. 1, then to Esperanza, where it is clamshelled from standard- to narrow gauge cars, and finally to Bach's Canyon.

Another standard-length passing track is at Belgrade, almost to the summit, and then we coast into Triple Divide Junction. Here, disguised as the parting of the ways that heads trains for either Hardscrabble or Golconda, is a wye which enables us to turn consists rapidly yet invisibly. In addition, layover tracks are provided so that up to three of our standard-length trains can readily be swallowed up to reappear later in any desired sequence as realistically as if they had actually gone all the way to the ends of our primarily imaginary railroad. If you don't mind a little less choice as to which comes out first, you can actually handle four at once.

The visible wye connection paralleling the hidden track is not strictly necessary but completely legitimate as the natural place to turn helpers for the trip back down the mountain. Its two turnouts are readily accessible, so it's easy to build, and it also serves to handle the occasional carload moving from one branch to the other. With only the single-ended spur available as an off-the-main roosting place, this last maneuver is still a worthy little switching puzzle you may have fun thinking about.

When one of those double-length jobs reaches Triple Divide, it must represent a consist of cars bound in approximately equal numbers for the two branches. It already has two engines, so motive power for the two pieces is available. With the pusher engine at hand to grab another caboose from the spur and provide a suitable tailpiece for the second train, it's a straightforward but interesting operation. The possibilities with respect to passenger trains are even more varied.

PRECAUTIONS AND VARIATIONS

This layout is actually designed on a rather conservative basis with 18" radius curves on the narrow gauge, which are approximately equivalent to 30" curves in standard gauge HO, 24- to 42-foot cars being typical of narrow gauge lines. As a little study of the Recommended Practices section of your NMRA Manual will show, the appropriate frog angle for your narrow gauge turnouts is at least no. 6, which still results in a compact little job only 4" from point to frog, and the plan allows room for these. Two-inch track centers are also allowed for, partly to make the plan suitable for standard gauge and also for appearance reasons. Even with code 70 rail, our narrow gauge model track will look considerably coarser in appearance than the prototype, but one of the things that identifies and gives that 3-foot gauge flavor to a scene (to me, at least) is that wide space between the two spindly tracks at a passing siding. To catch that feeling, using spacing even a bit wider than the NMRA's conservative standards (1⅝" minimum) on tangent track seems worthwhile.

As intimated before, this plan is also suitable, with little modification, for standard gauge HO. In this form, with its sharp curvature, it should move back in time to where Consolidations and Ten Wheelers were the big power of the day, and the tail tracks of the wye turnaround should be lengthened to hold a respectable number of 40-foot cars.

In On3, the railroad would fit very comfortably into the corresponding 22 x 24-foot space, and as a shelf-type affair would not become impractically wide. The one thing to watch would be elevation; a somewhat lower base level and more of a downgrade between Marlin and East Park would be called for to keep the summit from going right up against the ceiling. Aisle width, 24" minimum in HO, would become 48" or so for an O scale paraphrase of the plan. This is unnecessarily liberal. The extra space would better be used to expand the radius of the lower-level end loops to 54" or so to accommodate really big power on the main line. With the same considerations as mentioned for the HOn3-to-HO transformation, the track plan can become a satisfactory O scale period pike.

PROGRESSIVE CONSTRUCTION

In its general characteristics, this pike is of the "little gem" variety—a railroad which will never be known for its size but one on which there is ample opportunity to spend as many years as you have left in refining and superdetailing its many individual scenic and operating tidbits. This refining process is no fun if you must start in each case by correcting early substandard construction because you built too much track before starting operation. So an important consideration is the possibility of starting to operate at an early date, before the temptation to slap down the rest of the track becomes overpowering. Here this plan scores fairly well. First, there's the standard gauge dogbone, much of which will be out of sight forever and can be made from prefab sections of curvable track. This too is the stamping ground for the kitbuilt rolling stock that got you into the hobby in the first place.

At this point there is no need to build the peninsula in the center of the room that will eventually support the Bach's Canyon-Belgrade-Triple Divide territory. The narrow gauge construction can start at Esperanza but without the immediate necessity for any dual-gauge trackwork, unless your trackbuilding skills are already sharpened. From a track or two here you can proceed leisurely through Cameo Canyon and Marlin to East Park, where a temporary connection from A to B makes a loop that gets you fully, yet painlessly, into the business of running a lot of narrow gauge trains.

Later steps, such as adding the passing track at East Park, building and then bridging Sapsucker Creek, and starting the line up through Wigley, bring their own immediate rewards in stepped-up operating possibilities. By the time you must cover over Cameo Canyon to complete the main line, you have had time to get its scenery fully detailed, using your most highly developed techniques.

With the continually increasing room for slim gauge rolling stock the line provides, and the prospect that scratchbuilding will continue to be the norm in this field, it's your own fault if you get bored with this railroad.

The Allegheny Route

The story of the concept, the planning, the hardships, and

the rewards of building the Canandaigua Southern Railroad

DETAILED PLANNING of the Southern Division of the Canandaigua Southern ¼" scale, 1:48 began an hour after we had plunked down a payment on a suitable house in Silver Spring, Md. The delay, of course, was to avoid the appearance of unseemly haste after the 50-minute drive back to the apartment.

The requirements for the pike had developed over several years, including three smaller layout projects. Thus no time was lost in thinking them out:
• A main line long enough to give the feel of a real railroad.
• One fair-sized yard. A big hill.
• Quick-turn facilities at each end of the line.
• Et cetera—lots of et cetera, such as several passing tracks and a round-house for an already-built 134-foot articulated.

Other desires were negative but almost as essential: no short mainline circuits; no duckunders; no points where more than one section of main line would be visible. I wanted just one point-to-point route, mostly single

track. The inevitable paralleling sections of main line caused by doubling back the route to gain distance would either be hidden by a hill or backdrop, or else be located behind the engineer or train watcher walking alongside. I realized by now that some sort of spiral walk-in arrangement of the aisleways and benchwork would have to be it. Minimum radius would be at least 48", because that was the case on the Northern Division.

Canandaigua Southern's Northern Division, incidentally, had been in operation for a dozen years in its namesake community. "Cannon-day-gwuh," N.Y., is in the Finger Lakes region. The city is the terminal of Penn Central's subsidiary Northern Central Railway and is on the erstwhile New York Central's "Auburn Road" branch. I don't like to brag, but you'll find "Can Sou" stock listed on the New York Stock Exchange.

The first plans for the new layout were based on paced-off dimensions of the basement: 24 x 36 feet, give or take a foot or so. As fig. 1 shows, it turned out that, more or less regardless of the exact

radius, there could be no more than four parallel sections of benchwork at the critical point, opposite the internal turn-back lobe, in any 24-foot-wide space. This would still seem to allow for a respectably long main line. It did become clear that turning the trains at

─── *Author's Insight* ───

Since I have now lived with this track plan for 50 years, it would be embarrassing if I didn't feel that the railroad demonstrates several ideas of general usefulness. Otherwise, why haven't I discarded or rebuilt it in favor of something better?

What has developed in recent times as I've struggled to design a comparable amount of railroad into a somewhat equivalent area—about 25 square squares—is an appreciation for just how lucky I was to be blessed with, or to have hit upon, several key space-expanding factors:
• Entrance to a moderately oblong basement via a central stairway, absence of an outside door, and clearance behind

or between the utilities, permitting full use of all four walls
• Basic plan with a single spiral peninsula winding to stacked end loops filling the central area with once-around main line with only one space-eating "blob" of trackage
• Mountainous terrain allowing tracks, on opposite sides of a backdrop, to lap over each other at critical points—at the cost of a grossly excessive number of tunnels
• Full exploitation of the space-saving properties of curved turnouts, eased curves, and a sharp ladder angle

A good plan still needs sound implementation to achieve its full potential!

PAUL DOLKOS

the ends and corners of the benchwork would be the tricky part in matching my unreasonable desires to the unyielding space. If point-to-point is so great, why not just a straight terminal at each end? These would take no great width and would fit most anywhere. Fine, if the CS was to be a shortline operation—but it wasn't. By desire and by all existing rolling stock, it was already firmly committed to being a sort of Western Maryland or Clinchfield with more passengers. The "Allegheny Route," as the CS is often called, extends in theory from western New York state to Pittsburgh, doing it the hard way over the chopped-up plateau country of central northwestern Pennsylvania. The Southern Division was being planned in 1950, before we had ever heard the term "Appalachia" and realized that almost

every mile of the CS route was in an officially depressed area. Figure 2 shows the route. It doesn't explain just how the NYC was induced to short-route itself by setting up such solid working arrangements for through traffic. Maybe one of the early proprietors had some nefarious hold over Cornelius Vanderbilt.

The planning of a model railroad is a contest between space devoted to aisleways and benchwork, as already noted, and also between terminal space and main line. Should there be one terminal? Two? None? Not only the space a terminal requires, but also the time a man must spend in operating it, must be considered. In planning the CS it became apparent that to a big-time-railroading fan, most of the fun of operation must come from bridge traffic—

Steam-powered CS declines to overlook such spectaculars of the modern era as tank-hoppers, high-cubes, piggybacks, and tri-level racks.

people and tonnage loaded elsewhere and destined for somewhere else, yet now passing over the section of line actually modeled. It's fun to terminate a train in a stub yard, turn and rearrange it, and send the new consist on its way; but on a model railroad you can't do this quickly (or enjoyably) enough to satisfy the incessant demand of the main line for more and more trains. Besides, such an operation is true to life only for passenger trains in a fair-sized metropolis.

Moreover, model railroad yards, except in the case of large club layouts, tend to be picayunish condensations of the real thing. Trying to fit in, build, and

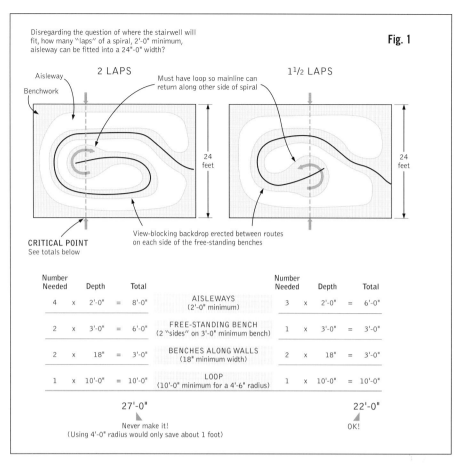

Disregarding the question of where the stairwell will fit, how many "laps" of a spiral, 2'-0" minimum, aisleway can be fitted into a 24"-0" width?

Fig. 1

2 LAPS

Aisleway
Benchwork
Must have loop so mainline can return along other side of spiral

1½ LAPS

24 feet

24 feet

CRITICAL POINT
See totals below

View-blocking backdrop erected between routes on each side of the free-standing benches

Number Needed		Depth		Total			Number Needed		Depth		Total
4	x	2'-0"	=	8'-0"	AISLEWAYS (2'-0" minimum)		3	x	2'-0"	=	6'-0"
2	x	3'-0"	=	6'-0"	FREE-STANDING BENCH (2 "sides" on 3'-0" minimum bench)		1	x	3'-0"	=	3'-0"
2	x	18"	=	3'-0"	BENCHES ALONG WALLS (18" minimum width)		2	x	18"	=	3'-0"
1	x	10'-0"	=	10'-0"	LOOP (10'-0" minimum for a 4'-6" radius)		1	x	10'-0"	=	10'-0"
				27'-0"							**22'-0"**

Never make it!
(Using 4'-0" radius would only save about 1 foot)

OK!

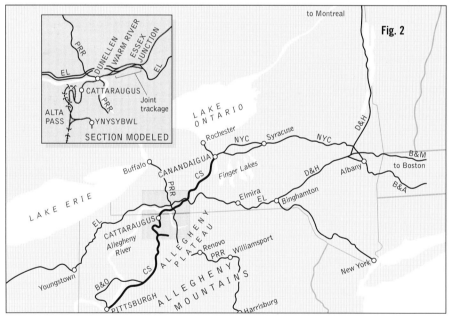

Fig. 2

to Montreal

SECTION MODELED

PRR — DUNELLEN — WARM RIVER — ESSEX JUNCTION — EL
CATTARAUGUS
PRR — Joint trackage
ALTA PASS
YNYSYBWL

LAKE ONTARIO

Rochester — NYC — Syracuse — NYC — D&H
B&M to Boston
Buffalo — CANANDAIGUA — CS — Finger Lakes — D&H — Albany
LAKE ERIE
EL — Elmira — EL — Binghamton — B&A
CATTARAUGUS
Allegheny River
ALLEGHENY PLATEAU
Renovo — Williamsport — New York
Youngstown — CS — PRR
B&O — ALLEGHENY MOUNTAINS
PITTSBURGH — Harrisburg

ment was ideally located, especially compared to a transverse one or one alongside an outside wall. (Either would have caused the whole house to be rejected.) The two columns supporting the center I beams were certainly as few and far between as was reasonable—after all, we do live upstairs. Nevertheless, one of them was precisely at the point of maximum inconvenience. You wouldn't think that one 6" steel column could make so much trouble in a 24 x 36-foot basement; but it did. One-track loops could dodge it easily enough, but when the added layover sidings were adjusted to clear the column, the whole scheme tended to blow up. For the moment I gave up putting the layovers in the loops.

The first serious design attempt was based on the rational scheme shown in fig. 4. It is included here for whatever inspiration it might be to someone with an open mind, similar requirements, and a situation perhaps more conducive to actual construction of "The Hole." The single-ended tail tracks were to be located in a sealed pipe extending almost 20 feet under the back yard, in this case, at a depth just below the 18" frost line in this area. Knocking the required hole through the basement wall being an imaginative and laborious matter at best, the tunnel was planned to accommodate four trains on two levels, thus hopefully making the agony of creation worthwhile. Very little operating or maintenance trouble was anticipated, because the portion of the trackage inside the bowels of the earth would be straight, devoid of turnouts, and non-powered. All trains would back, engine last, into the tomb and subsequently be revived for their return journeys.

A genuinely promising plan based on this concept was completed. There were some awkward matters, such as a yard location which kept running afoul of the only logical laundry location, but a 230-foot main line resulted. It had 54" minimum radius, five passing locations, and excellent scenic possibilities. Fortunately, before 20 feet of corrugated iron culvert was ordered, a way was found to make the original stacked-loop scheme fit the space. The whole hole idea was put aside with relief, the new plan emerged, and construction started in November 1950. The diagrams in fig. 5 and the main drawing on page 50 show the railroad as it is today. The track plan has changed only in detail over the intervening years.

maintain two end-of-line yards couldn't help but make each of them smaller and more pitiful than to have only one. Anyway, only a masochist would be overjoyed at the prospect of going through the track-building process twice. The solution for the CS was to have the ends of the line represented by hidden terminal loops plus some layover trackage so that trains would not

have to come back in the same sequence. Even at that rudimentary stage it was also clear that, to make reasonable use of the space, the two loops should be stacked one above the other, and that they would have to be located in the center of the basement. So fig. 3 was the first concept. It looked at first as if everything would fit nicely.

The stairway coming into the base-

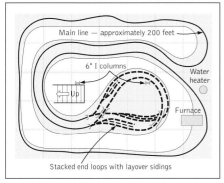

Fig. 3

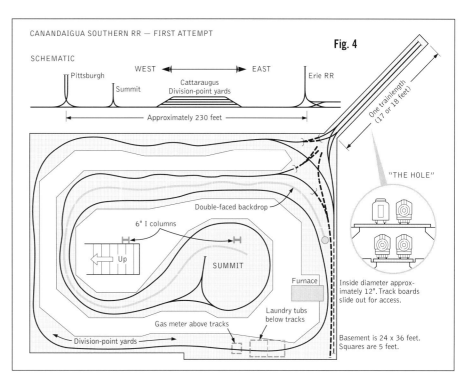

CANANDAIGUA SOUTHERN RR — FIRST ATTEMPT

Fig. 4

THE REVERTED LOOP

The key to the successful plan was a "reverted" loop used to turn trains at the west, or Pittsburgh, end of the main line: fig. 6. This met the challenge of the steel column by relocating the layover trackage. Only a single loop track needed to snake its way past the post. Figure 7 shows it in detail. The arrangement concealed the layover and turn-around trackage without unduly shortening the visible main line. The practicability of this had to be taken on faith, though, because the reverted loop couldn't be built until the rest of the main line was operating. This took 8 years—thus making the elapsed-time building of the project almost half again as impressive as the Union Pacific-Central Pacific feat, which took 6 years. The CS can't claim to be as wide or as long as the Overland Route, but our roadbed was a lot better seasoned than theirs!

As you can deduce from fig. 5, westbound trains which have conquered the hill proceed past Altapass into Tunnel no. 5, ending the visible part of their journey to Pittsburgh. Once out of sight—see fig. 7—they continue counterclockwise until the last car has cleared the throat at A. The engineer determines this from his control station by watching through the tunnel mouth: fig. 8. Since the CS has outside-third-rail distribution, it would have been an easy matter to use a track circuit to do the same job in a classier fashion, but cutting a hole in the far side of the mountain to provide a silhouette of the caboose was even easier—so that's the way it was done. The hole also allows removing any trash that may get into the turnout points.

The hidden switch is reversed and the train then backs up the 1.4 percent grade, taking the sharp side of the turnout and immediately starting down the 4 percent "Loop" track. Backing

through Troat, the consist eases its way into an open layover track in the Dotsero "subway." Once in this hidden yard, trains are considered eastbound. They can subsequently emerge from Tunnel no. 5, via the left side of turnout B, in any desired order. If all three Dotsero tracks are full when the dispatcher sends another westbound past Altapass, the shortest train—if no longer than 14 cars—can use the track at Loop, waiting there until another train departs and leaves a slot for it. With the crossover between tracks 1 and 2 at Dotsero, it's theoretically possible to have six trains out of sight at this end of the line. In practice this hasn't been done. We never seem to run enough short trains to fit two to a track.

As you can see from the profile in fig. 5, fitting the tail of the reverted loop into the vertical space between the lower loop (Idden) and the top level (Altapass wye) was a fairly tight proposition at best. Eliminating the wye would have greatly eased the problem, but also it would have eliminated much of the realism of the classic helper-district operation between the turntable at Cattaraugus and the out-in-the-open loco-turning facility at the top of the hill. The mine spur leading from the wye (at no extra charge) eventually developed into a short but relatively full-fledged branchline operation to Ynysybwl; this would have been considerably limited in scope without the complete wye. Thus the loop's 4 percent pitch was

accepted in the design—recognizing, of course, that trains need go only downhill on this track.

PLANNED UNBALANCE; AN EXTRA GOODY

Grades on the main line had definite requirements to fill. The "big hill" was to be long enough to give a pusher engine a sense of purpose and accomplishment. The "river division" east of the division point was to be level enough, by contrast, to require—or at least justify—a change in motive-power characteristics between the two ends of the railroad. Experience with previous layouts had shown that considerable exaggeration of prototype grades is necessary to get the right feel. On the hill, something on the order of a 3 or 3.5 percent grade was the target for the westbound grade. A markedly lighter grade was used eastbound out of the "Pittsburgh" layover trackage so that trains which had dropped their helpers could return without assistance. On the river division, Pacifics and Hudsons should be able to handle trains brought to Cattaraugus by 4-8-4s and articulateds. Grades here were kept well below 1 percent. This made it logical to locate the principal engine terminal of the railroad at this central division point, with passenger power working out-and-back assignments in the way the N&W ran its Js out of Roanoke. Cattaraugus roundhouse would be no rival to the size of Shaffer's Crossing, but it would

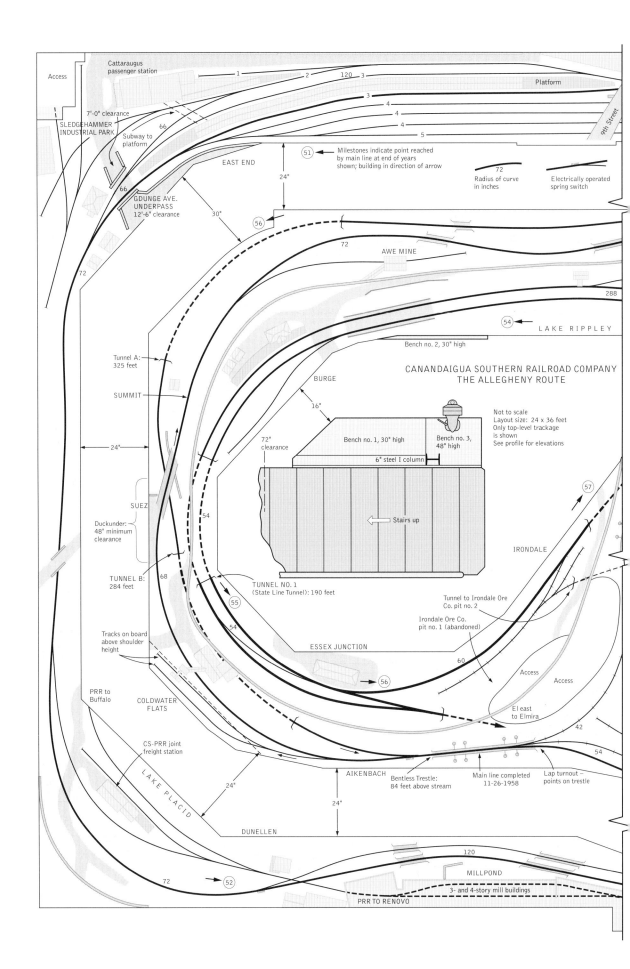

Access

Cattaraugus
passenger station

1

2   120   3

Platform

3

4

4

4

5

7'-0" clearance

SLEDGEHAMMER
INDUSTRIAL PARK

Subway to
platform

66

EAST END

51 ── Milestones indicate point reached
by main line at end of years
shown; building in direction of arrow

72
Radius of curve
in inches

Electrically operated
spring switch

24"

66

GDUNGE AVE.
UNDERPASS
12'-6" clearance

30"

56

72

AWE MINE

288

72

54   ← LAKE RIPPLEY

Bench no. 2, 30" high

Tunnel A:
325 feet

BURGE

CANANDAIGUA SOUTHERN RAILROAD COMPANY
THE ALLEGHENY ROUTE

SUMMIT

16"

Not to scale
Layout size: 24 x 36 feet
Only top-level trackage
is shown
See profile for elevations

24"

72"
clearance

Bench no. 1, 30" high

Bench no. 3,
48" high

6" steel I column

57

SUEZ

Duckunder:
48" minimum
clearance

54

Stairs up

IRONDALE

TUNNEL B:
284 feet

68

TUNNEL NO. 1
(State Line Tunnel): 190 feet

55

Tunnel to Irondale Ore
Co. pit no. 2

Irondale Ore Co.
pit no. 1 (abandoned)

54

ESSEX JUNCTION

Tracks on board
above shoulder
height

60

Access

Access

56

PRR to
Buffalo

COLDWATER
FLATS

El east
to Elmira

42

CS-PRR joint
freight station

24"

AIKENBACH

Bentless Trestle:
84 feet above stream

Main line completed
11-26-1958

Lap turnout –
points on trestle

54

L A K E   P L A C I D

24"

DUNELLEN

120

MILLPOND

72

52

3- and 4-story mill buildings

PRR TO RENOVO

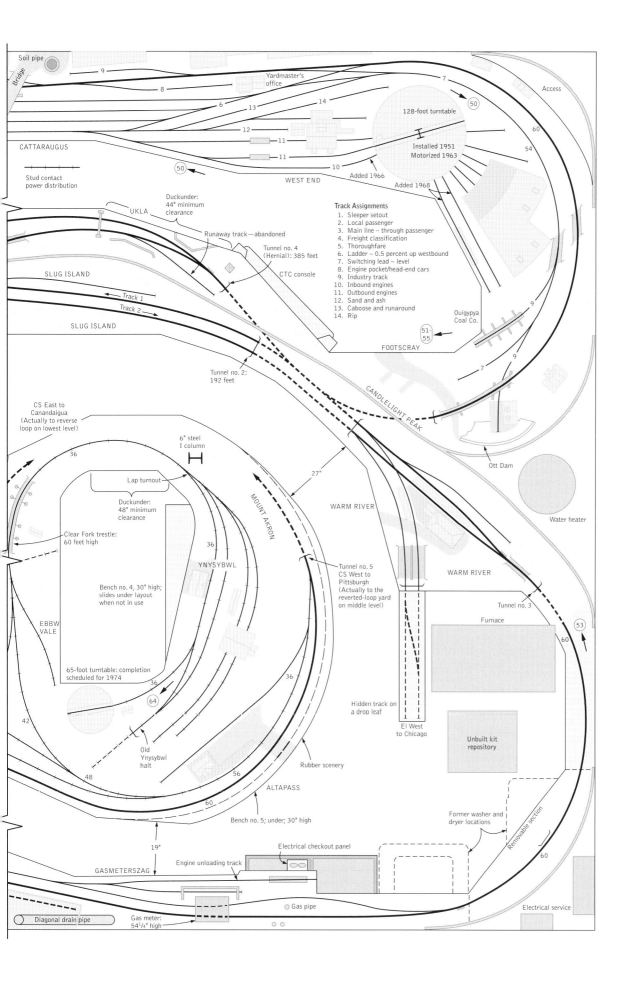

Soil pipe

Bridge

9

8

Yardmaster's office

7

Access

6

13

14

50

60

12

54

11

CATTARAUGUS

11

128-foot turntable

Installed 1951
Motorized 1963

50

10

Added 1966

WEST END

Added 1968

Track Assignments
1. Sleeper setout
2. Local passenger
3. Main line – through passenger
4. Freight classification
5. Thoroughfare
6. Ladder – 0.5 percent up westbound
7. Switching lead – level
8. Engine pocket/head-end cars
9. Industry track
10. Inbound engines
11. Outbound engines
12. Sand and ash
13. Caboose and runaround
14. Rip

Stud contact
power distribution

Duckunder:
44" minimum
clearance

UKLA

Runaway track—abandoned

Tunnel no. 4
(Hernial): 385 feet

CTC console

Ouigypya
Coal Co.

9

SLUG ISLAND

51-
55

FOOTSCRAY

7

9

Track 1

Track 2

SLUG ISLAND

Tunnel no. 2:
192 feet

CANDLELIGHT PEAK

CS East to
Canandaigua
(Actually to reverse
loop on lowest level)

36

6" steel
I column

H

27"

Ott Dam

Lap turnout

Duckunder:
48" minimum
clearance

WARM RIVER

Water heater

Clear Fork trestle:
60 feet high

36

YNYSYBWL

Tunnel no. 5
CS West to
Pittsburgh
(Actually to the
reverted-loop yard
on middle level)

WARM RIVER

Bench no. 4, 30" high;
slides under layout
when not in use

36

Tunnel no. 3

53

EBBW
VALE

Furnace

60

65-foot turntable: completion
scheduled for 1974

36

36

64

Hidden track on
a drop leaf

42

El West
to Chicago

Unbuilt kit
repository

48

Old
Ynysybwl
halt

56

Rubber scenery

ALTAPASS

60

Former washer and
dryer locations

Bench no. 5; under; 30" high

19"

GASMETERSZAG

Electrical checkout panel

Engine unloading track

Removable section

60

Electrical service

Diagonal drain pipe

Gas pipe

Gas meter:
54¼" high

definitely be too big for the rest of the layout without some such gimmick in the operating plan.

As it turned out, some practical considerations governed the track elevations just as that one steel column had determined the track plan. The height of the railroad was set by the necessity of passing directly beneath the gas meter, between a gas pipe and the cellar wall. The meter was already mounted as high against the joists as its piping allowed, so the main line at this point could be precisely 50″ above the floor and still let the 4-6-6-6 have ¼″ clearance above its 16-foot stack. It wasn't even possible to dodge the little feet embossed in the bottom of the meter and thus pick up another ¼″. Just beyond the meter, eastbound, a short but sharp grade a bit over 1.5 percent got the line high enough to let the washing machine lid serve its purpose. The little Hungarian town of Gasmeterszag was thus located.

HOW HIGH THE HILL?

As an elevation for the river division and the yards, 49″ is a little lower than I like, but still a big improvement over the 36″ and 42″ heights around a meter on my earlier layouts. The elevation of the main line at what is now Altapass was limited to 63″ by the fact that it would have to come directly below a heating duct. Even with the shortest available longnose pliers it's an uncomfortable squint job pushing in spikes within 12″ of the overhead; yet laid-in-place track is to be preferred when so many curved turnouts, easements, and superelevated curves are involved.

Even so, the 14″ rise required almost 60 feet at an average of 2 percent, and the hill wouldn't be something you could overcome just by getting a good running start. To make it more interesting, the main line splits into two routes along here. The original "high" line climbs at 3.5 percent for some 35 feet to reach Summit at 65″ elevation. The newer "low" line with its expensive tunnels, built in theory in the late 1930s, reaches its apex farther along at Aikenbach by climbing at 2 percent. It has a little flattening in the tunnels where this can't be seen. A feature of this part of the CS is the flyover of the old line over the new, patterned after the Santa Fe-Union Pacific trick just east of Cajon Pass. [Going east, the two railroads climb a canyon to the summit. In the bottom of the ravine is the original Santa Fe track taking a steep grade.

Higher on the left as you go up is the Union Pacific track taking an easy grade. Both railroads use the easy track for the climb, and return on the steep grade. This makes this part of their systems left-hand running, but a few miles beyond the summit there is a flyover to restore the jointly used tracks to right-hand running.]

On the CS the westbound trains normally use their new line in the same way, with double-track rules in effect between Ukla and Aikenbach. There is a stretch of 3.5 percent for all trains from Cattaraugus through Hernial Tunnel. Plenty of road power or a "short pusher" out of the division point is still the rule for everything headed west.

As mentioned earlier, an easier eastbound grade out of Dotsero, representing Pittsburgh, was highly desirable to give an unbalanced tractive-force requirement between the two sides of the big hill and thus let most eastbound trains return without helpers. After considerable juggling and calculating, a steady 1.4 percent grade extending for 73 feet from Dotsero through Altapass and Summit was worked out. With this done, the critical phase of planning was over.

The main objectives had been met with a main line that definitely would fit horizontally and vertically. Construction could start with assurance—assuming, of course, that trains could back through the adverse grades and curves of the reverted loop successfully.

Prospects were dim for acquiring any new rail in 1951. Materials restrictions during the Korean War had considerable bite to them, as modelers who tried to use steel rails for HO layouts will remember. So the total trackage in the plan was estimated carefully. It came to 690 feet, of which perhaps 175 feet could be deferred while still pushing the main line to completion. I had about 400 feet of assorted rail on hand and could count on cannibalizing another 650 feet from the still-operating Northern Division if necessary.

THE RAILROAD THAT WALKED, AND OTHER STORIES

The plan has a defect which might have been a real problem under different circumstances. It provides no way to get part of the line into full service at an early stage of construction. This did not really hurt in this case, both because of occasional visits to the Northern Division and because Cattaraugus Yard, built first, offered pretty fair operating

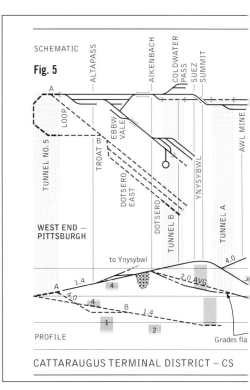

SCHEMATIC

Fig. 5

WEST END — PITTSBURGH

PROFILE

CATTARAUGUS TERMINAL DISTRICT – CS

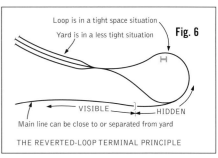

Loop is in a tight space situation

Yard is in a less tight situation

Fig. 6

VISIBLE — HIDDEN

Main line can be close to or separated from yard

THE REVERTED-LOOP TERMINAL PRINCIPLE

possibilities by itself. To make construction more pleasant, that yard was built temporarily 1½ feet away from the wall so it could be worked on from both sides. Benchwork and trackage were built as far west of Cattaraugus as Footscray, so that full-length cuts of cars could be classified. The construction gangs next started east along the river division. The work progressed as indicated by the chronological "mileposts" on the main drawing, page 50. With only occasional lapses, a resolution to spike all track fully before moving to the next section was observed.

In due course the main line reached a point approaching Warm River, where its benchwork would be common with that supporting the proposed west-end line through Hernial Tunnel. Before this could proceed, Cattaraugus Yard would have to be moved into its final position against the wall. By now it was attached to a stretch of layout almost 100 feet long, supported on 26 legs. With some foresight the framework between the

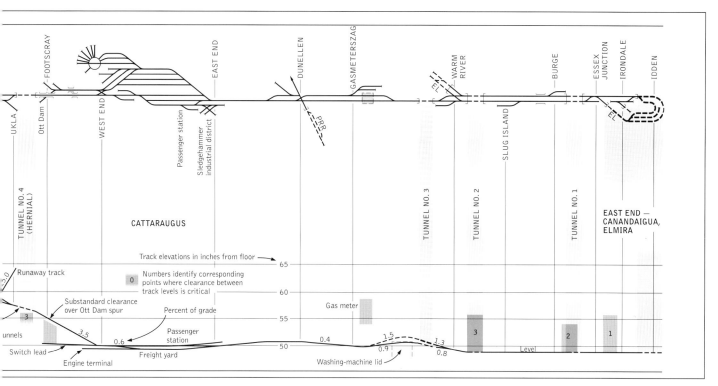

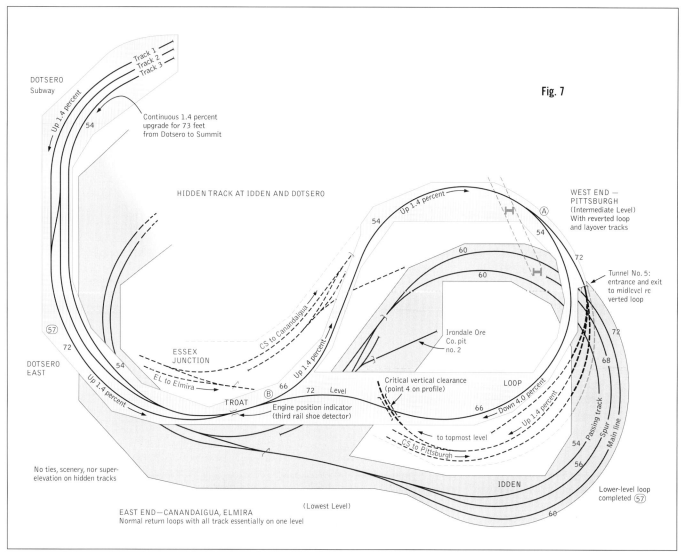

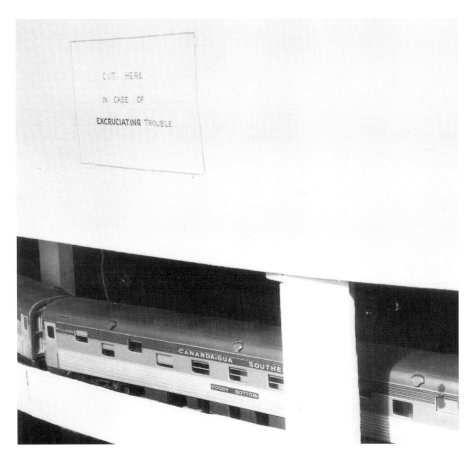

Fig. 8. The east end layover trackage at Idden, on the lowest level, is accessible but is normally in the dark and fairly inconspicuous. The reverting loop track above it is completely boxed in at this point. So far it has had no hangups in meeting the emergency-access criterion.

east end of Cattaraugus and Dunellen had been bolted together with an 18" overlap in the side rails, but the whole section to be moved looked like it might not withstand flexing in the moving process without some damage.

At this point the social advantages of model railroading became profitable. The Metropolitan Society of Model Engineers of nearby Washington, D.C., came for a visit in sufficient strength so that one member could be assigned to each layout leg. The expandable section was unbolted, and at the call of "One, two, three, KICK," each leg was moved an inch or so at a time. The railroad was walked into position with no pain nor strain. A prefabricated chunk of main-line track was dropped into the gap; and before it was time for coffee, trains were once more running to the end of track and back.

The main line continued its gradual extension. We laid about 100 feet of track per year in those days, and service was maintained on a shuttle basis. This was satisfying operation and an ideal test of the trackwork. With precisely half of the train mileage run cars first,

engine last, defects will show up promptly. Despite the proximity of almost all trackage to the edge of the layout, engineers soon developed confidence. Full-length consists were backed for miles at normal speeds. This was just as the Chicago & North Western used to run some of its commuter trains to their starting points every morning. The relatively few accidents were usually of a unique nature: double rear-end collisions in which the boat-tail of the *Smoky City Limited* would enter an overlooked open turnout and clout the caboose of a coal drag. [CNW's push-pull commuter trains have a diesel at one end and controls at both ends.]

Benchwork and train progressed in the center of the room. After 1957, when the lower-level loop at Idden was completed, a train could run for some 300 feet—from one end of the line, around the loop, and back. Then, of course, it still had 300 feet of backing to do before repeating the process. Nevertheless, operations became more fun, and construction tended to slow appreciably.

Before the trackage up the big hill beyond Awl Mine could be put in place

it was necessary to start construction of the isolated Dotsero tail tracks and the reverted loop trackage: fig. 7. Since the test-as-you-build philosophy was firmly in force, the railroad was now operating as two disconnected segments.

On the principal section heading up the 3.5 percent we were finding that engines (at least in ¼" scale) keep getting more and more powerful as they get older. The single-powered diesel switcher, lettered LACKAWANNA & ERIE because the CS is all-steam, had trouble handling cuts of 10 cars on the slight grade of the Cattaraugus switch lead when first built. Now it was handling 16 cars with ease. CS's 4-8-4 took the standard full-length freight—17 cars as determined by most of the siding lengths—up the high line unassisted. This indicated that helpers might be more decorative than essential.

On the relatively short Dotsero-Troat-Altapass section, the moment of truth was approaching. Would the reverted-loop idea work? By this time it had appeared in a track plan article in the September 1954 issue of *Model Railroader*. Several years had gone by with no complaints; but this didn't mean anything, because new ideas in magazine features sometimes take a long, long time to be put into practice. Furthermore, as it said in the article, any sensible person would make sure the backing maneuver was downhill, or at least on the level, and through the straight side of the facing-point turnout. The same author [Armstrong is being modest here] also emphasized that only an idiot would not provide ready access to all track and turnouts involved in such a hairy procedure. By this time, this particular idiot, having already committed himself to shoving 'em backward up a 1.4 percent grade and through the sharp side of a minimum-radius curved turnout, was now planning to extend the Altapass wye into a branch, with scenery that would cover the whole works. You might say that access was provided for, but not on an instant basis: fig. 8.

THE RUSTY STEEL SPIKE

By the time the reverted-loop trackage was to be covered, it had been established that trains could take such trackage reliably, even if the percentage play would be to avoid such challenges. There are rules in the timecard that discourage putting light cars near the head end of mountain division consists. The loop is always traversed in clockwise fashion so we at least stay away from backing up a 4 percent grade. "Reverting" on the CS has become a routine movement not much different from running around a conventional wye in flat country.

By October 19, 1969, only the track on Bentless Trestle between Aikenbach and Altapass was needed to complete the main line. The importance of this segment was emphasized when a stub mail and express train which had been backed up the hill as far as possible, with the "two railroads" operating scheme still in effect, started its run to Cattaraugus and the river division. Unfortunately, the controls were in reverse motion. Tunnels A and B hid this fact; the locomotive assigned had plenty of power to move tile train uphill, and those waiting near Ukla to see it emerge from the tunnel were shocked to hear, instead, a loud "plop-plop-plop-crunch!" as the last four cars were pushed vigorously into the abyss.

From then on, construction was more rapid. By October 26 the track was in place. On November 26 the main line went into operation unofficially. There never has been a proper gold spike ceremony. Incidentally, the bridge is strong enough even without center bents to carry 25-pound locomotives, so the engineering department never did finish the drawings for these frills. The Commemorative Commission in turn is too embarrassed to contemplate public exhibition of such an obviously incompleted part of the railroad—so the ceremony waits: fig. 9.

TRACK PLAN CHANGES

Once the main line was in service, lesser trackage was completed at a leisurely rate. The steadily increasing roster of rolling stock supplied gentle but constant pressure to add spurs wherever practical. The actual railroad, fortunately, looks considerably bigger in the flesh than on paper, so it was possible to put extra trackage at several points without unduly crowding things. The Ynysybwl colliery loading tracks were extended to eight-car lengths. A second spur was found to be feasible at Coldwater Flats because the line is high enough at that point to clear almost anyone's shoulder; thus the extra track doesn't really narrow the aisleway. The fake junction trackage with the Pennsy at Dunellen was extended to include a short hidden

Fig. 9. Even without center bents, the bridge is strong enough to carry a 25-pound locomotive!

runaround which considerably enhances operating possibilities. The turntable was motorized in 1963. Without it there was too much congestion when the railroad really got going. The third engine terminal track was extended to the turntable shortly (3 years) afterward.

The only modification to the original mainline plan was double-tracking the section between Burge and Essex Junction. Had the original scheme been followed, the line would have been definitely more single-track in character, but Essex Junction's trackage would

have been less interesting. It also would have created a bottleneck at what should be, in theory, the heaviest traffic section of the route. Despite the modesty of the changes, we gained over 300 feet of trackage. The last rail, in probability, is now down; and the 690 feet originally estimated has become an actual 1000 feet.

The Carlsbad, East Portal & Zenith Railroad

A lot of N scale railroading in 4 x 8 feet, and

designed to hang from the ceiling!

BECAUSE THE Carlsbad, East Portal & Zenith will be required to handle fairly large motive power and long trains in minimum area, in it I've departed from the out-and-back schematic I usually favor for providing a good mix of terminal switching and mainline running in a space equivalent to about three by five squares. Since its proprietor wants it to be a "railroad in suspension"—up against the ceiling between operating and building sessions but accessible from all sides when in the lowered position—it can have a hidden lower level underlying most of its topside area.

At 4 x 8 feet all areas of the layout are accessible from the edges, while N scale greatly magnifies the "one sheet of plywood" space. Even such massive locomotives as Santa Fe 4-8-4s are expected to (and do!) go around sharp curves in N. A 13" radius (equivalent to a conventional bend of about 24" in HO) is enough to ensure reliable operation in most cases. As it turns out, it's possible to raise the ante to 14½" for at least one track throughout the main line and for most layover tracks. If the CEP&Z should ultimately have some power that is picky about 13" curves, the big engines will still be able to make it around the railroad with some attention on the part of the dispatcher in planning their routing.

The appearance of the *Limited's* 85-foot passenger cars and of long-overhang engines will still suffer somewhat, of course, so more generous curves have been used wherever possible.

The worst of the bends will presumably be made less obvious by judicious location of scenic features and structures. A thoroughly prototypical curve extends right through Elm Grove, the one principal passenger station which the layout can afford, and it's right up front where all the good things it does for the train watcher are most readily appreciated.

Author's Insight

Once you're past the task of devising and installing a suitable suspension system, the layout hanging from the overhead has attractive features:
- The space it occupies remains usable for other purposes.
- The structural rigidity required translates into sound trackwork, enhancing operational reliability and appearance.
- The railroad can always be at an optimum height, for construction, for viewing, etc.

Four-by-eight layouts aren't usually noted for extensive staging, but with a single-turn helix and the hill-climbing reputation of early N gauge consists to gain altitude, the Carlsbad, East Portal & Zenith features two decks separated by the necessary hands-breadth; the lower level accommodates secluded looped-siding layover for six trains. This "yard" is accessible from the side also, comfortably from below, thanks to a large opening in the bottom plywood panel.

Topside, a hidden (but similarly accessible) upper-level loop makes the railroad a point-to-point affair. Since the whole thing will normally be at a proper near-eye-level during operation, terrain supporting the lofty Skytop mine branch provides scenic separation between the two sides of the layout that's sufficient to avoid a Christmas-tree appearance.

ONCE AGAIN, A HELIX

Given these concessions it becomes possible to meet requirements for operation and layover of fairly long trains by going to the one practical way of building a two-layer pike in such severely limited space: a helix. This separates the levels by about 4"—plenty so far as the height of N scale rolling stock is concerned, but just about the absolute minimum finger space required for taking care of the inevitable (though 'tis hoped rare) operational incidents. This plan isn't for a mountain-climbing railroad with helper engines as a big part of the fun, and the 3 percent grades in the helix should be no problem for most N scale trains because traction tires are common and the engine-to-car weight ratio is high.

As cross section A-A shows, access to the helix has to be from below, but that's no problem, since the railroad can simply be hauled up toward the ceiling to make this not only possible but almost comfortable. The lower-level layover trackage is likewise accessible from both an interior hole and from the outside. All turnouts have been carefully kept close to the exterior, even to some extent at the expense of layover-track length. The CEP&Z should nonetheless be able to run at least one freight in the 30- to 40-car range without completely immobilizing all other traffic on the railroad.

STRUCTURAL DESIGN MATTERS

It goes without saying that the structural design of a railroad like this is not a casual matter. Added to the require-

AT&SF 2-8-0 Consolidation no. 1987 arrives in Hemet, California, on September 12, 1946.

ment that the whole business float up into the stratosphere (powered by a garage-door opener mechanism) is a top-to-bottom height restriction of about a foot, to provide sufficient under-the-layout clearance when the room is being used for other purposes.

Essentially, the rigidity needed for a suspended railroad must come from the I-beam effect of the basic structural grid sandwiched between the plywood layers that form the upper and lower track supports. Particularly in N scale, any flexing will be very apparent in terms of the size of the trains.

Building the CEP&Z presumes planning the structure completely before

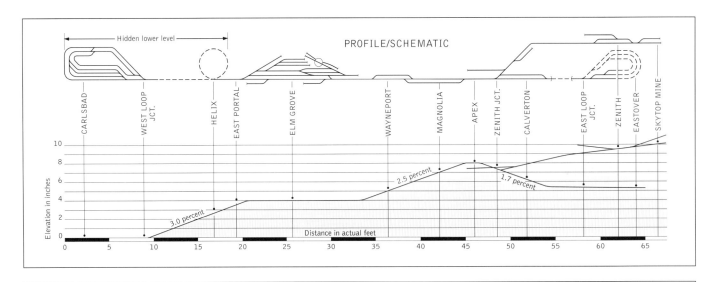

PROFILE/SCHEMATIC

Hidden lower level

CARLSBAD · WEST LOOP JCT. · HELIX · EAST PORTAL · ELM GROVE · WAYNEPORT · MAGNOLIA · APEX · ZENITH JCT. · CALVERTON · EAST LOOP JCT. · ZENITH · EASTOVER · SKYTOP MINE

Elevation in inches

3.0 percent

2.5 percent

1.7 percent

Distance in actual feet

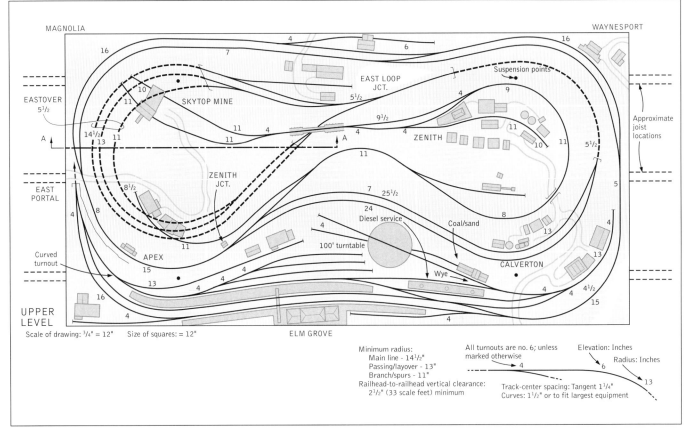

MAGNOLIA

WAYNESPORT

EASTOVER
5½

EAST LOOP JCT.

Suspension points

Approximate joist locations

SKYTOP MINE

ZENITH

A — A

EAST PORTAL

ZENITH JCT.

Curved turnout

APEX

Diesel service

100' turntable

Coal/sand

Wye

CALVERTON

UPPER LEVEL

ELM GROVE

Scale of drawing: ¾" = 12"   Size of squares: = 12"

Minimum radius:
  Main line - 14½"
  Passing/layover - 13"
  Branch/spurs - 11"
Railhead-to-railhead vertical clearance:
  2½" (33 scale feet) minimum

All turnouts are no. 6; unless marked otherwise

Elevation: Inches
Radius: Inches

Track-center spacing: Tangent 1¼"
Curves: 1½" or to fit largest equipment

GIVENS & DRUTHERS
Carlsbad, East Portal & Zenith RR.

Scale: N
Gauge: Std.
Prototype: Era: Late steam-present
                Region: Unspecified—mountains
                Railroad: Eclectic
Space: 4 x 8 feet, free-standing pull-down "island";
            suspended from ceiling; four suspension points

Governing rolling stock:
       4-8-4 locomotives
       85' dome passenger cars

Relative Emphasis:
       Operation and scenic realism
       Tends toward mainline running
Operating Priorities:
       1. Medium-length freight (10-15 cars)
       2. Mainline passenger (8-10 cars)
       3. Long freight train operation (>20 cars)
       4. Commuter trains (traffic)
       5. Local freight operations
Typical operating crew: One

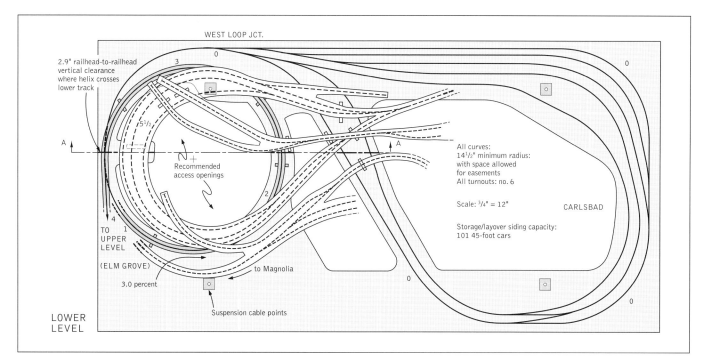

WEST LOOP JCT.

2.9" railhead-to-railhead vertical clearance where helix crosses lower track

Recommended access openings

All curves: 14½" minimum radius: with space allowed for easements
All turnouts: no. 6

Scale: ¾" = 12"

CARLSBAD

Storage/layover siding capacity: 101 45-foot cars

TO UPPER LEVEL

(ELM GROVE)

3.0 percent

to Magnolia

Suspension cable points

LOWER LEVEL

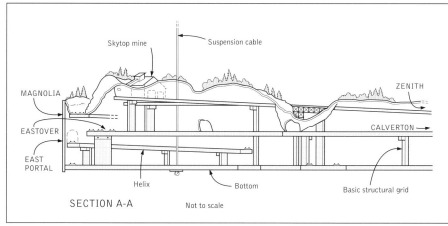

Skytop mine

Suspension cable

MAGNOLIA

ZENITH

EASTOVER

CALVERTON

EAST PORTAL

Helix

Bottom

Basic structural grid

SECTION A-A   Not to scale

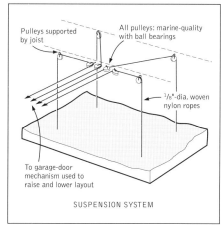

Pulleys supported by joist

All pulleys: marine-quality with ball bearings

⅛"-dia. woven nylon ropes

To garage-door mechanism used to raise and lower layout

SUSPENSION SYSTEM

taking saber saw to the virgin 4 x 8 plywood sheets, then working from the bottom up to lay, check out (by operation), and wire the hidden track. The nice part is that on a pike of this scope there isn't all that much to be done before the golden spike can be pushed into place.

LANDSCAPE AMONG THE JOISTS

Some scenery can rise up into the spaces between the overhead joists, and the Zenith/Skytop trackage has been located to take advantage of joist locations. As in any small, island-type track plan, it's extremely desirable that the terrain rise high enough along the central spine of the layout to separate the two sides visually, and the extra few inches between the joist locations can ensure success in this respect. If the situation is marginal, rubber trees

atop the ridge are always a possibility!

The CEP&Z's builder also included a cosmetic requirement that the underside of the suspended platform be reasonably presentable. This can be met by keeping the access-opening segments cut from the lower-level plywood sheet and arranging them to slide over and hide the gaping wounds.

A PRACTICAL RAILROAD – IN NO SPACE

With all this complexity, what's practical in 4 x 8 feet? Thanks to the wonders of 1/160 scale, the main line stretches almost two scale miles from loop to loop, there is on-track capacity for hiding 100 cars or so in the "basement" (although this will still be primarily a "sampler" railroad, on which only a selection of the owner's extensive roster will be operating at any given time),

and the Magnolia/Wayneport lap sidings allow considerable flexibility in handling long and short trains in a variety of traffic patterns. For a net space requirement (exclusive occupancy, that is) of zero, not too bad!

The Rio Grande Southern Railroad

A sit-in HOn3 layout to be built in a small room

NO DOUBT about it – this railroad is going to fall into the "little gem" category. Given rigid walls enclosing a 6'-8" x 8'-8" space and the proprietor's desire to emphasize realistic scenes rather than a complete jumble of track, the plan is going to be simple enough to permit superdetailing the whole thing—and that includes track, bridges, structures, rolling stock, lighting, sound effects, the works!

ACHIEVING VERTICAL SEPARATION

Even with the door to the room rehung to swing outward, there's not going to be room to use a two-level design in a scenically plausible arrangement—you could get up to an upper deck with a helix, but there would be no way to get back down without real crowding. What comes to the rescue is the prototype. Rio Grande Southern mainline grades, which started at a stiff 2.5 percent and increased to 4 percent on the approaches to Dallas Divide (along with many 24 degree curves—that's a 31" radius in HO scale), were just starters. Some of the mine branches were steep! So, choosing to model the RGS does legitimately make possible the maximum vertical separation between tracks which simply can't be kept as far apart in the horizontal direction as realism would otherwise demand.

Our latter-day HOn3 RGS comes with the requirement for motive power as big as a K-27 Mikado, so a 20" minimum mainline radius (with easements) is appropriate. That's tight, but not so skimpy as to require disfiguring modifications to achieve reliable operation with the big engine. So, the room size is equal to about 3½ x 4½ squares. A "waterwings" main line is about all that will fit, but that achieves a major goal: a walk-in railroad, rather than a doughnut-with-duckunder affair. Over the years, the person-feet of accumulated bending over that will be avoided will be monumental!

THE SIT-IN ALCOVE

The aisle in this layout—it's really more of an alcove—won't be up to normal minimum standards (24" to 30") so the RGS has evolved as more of a sit-in

Author's Insight

Narrow gauge, the ultimate in scenic ruggedness and, with its Galloping Geese, in run-lengthening short train consists, the Rio Grande Southern is a clear choice as an inspiration for a compact model railroad. Still, what can you do within a room too small to accommodate a slender railroader and even a 4 x 8 or a doughnut plan worth the duckunder?

Accepting the fact that this model railroad will at best be a generic rather than a condensed specific-segment representation of the RGS, a sit-in variant of the time-honored "waterwings" or "bow-tie" track plan should do.

With a 20" HOn3 radius giving us about 16 square squares to squander, an out-and-back schematic from a stub terminal to a continuous-run loop will fit. With one direction-reversing connection so located as to enforce a minimum twice-around trip, it should provide a fair mix of switching and running. In the confines of the room, though, there may be access problems within those two blobs in the back corners. Palliatives:
• Typical highly vertical RGS scenery comes to the rescue. In the foreground, open-back 3-D terrain can provide unobtrusive emergency access from below.
• A low (36"?) layout elevation, acceptable when running trains seated, makes "arm's length reach" longer when standing up.

Rio Grande Southern engine no. 20 pauses at Rico, Colorado.

design. The layout height shown is based on a pleasant eye-level view when operating from a seated position in the alcove, with the scenery and upper levels of track towering above in true San Juan country fashion. Stand up, and access to most trackage is fair to good so far as operation is concerned (although a couple of non-prototypical switch machines at Ophir and Hesperus Junction will be preferable to the hand-throws that are the first choice at foreground points). The backdrop will have to go up before the railroad is filled in, though.

What about subsequent minor maintenance, such as touching up scraped rock should something derail? Because the viewing angle is severely restricted, the back faces of most of the mountains

can be left open for easy, if moderately uncomfortable, access from below.

AN OUT-AND-BACK SCHEMATIC

The schematic is the one which is almost always the best possible for any pike built in an area of about 15 squares where you want any mainline running at all: out-and-back, from a stub terminal to a continuous-run oval with single reversing connection. Tracks in the stub yard can be longer than those in any yard directly on a continuous-run route, and the stub provides one point which must be operated as a terminal with all the switching that implies.

The necessarily short main line can be traversed as many times as desired before peeling off to the yard to again go

through the required stub-terminal moves. With proper placement of the branchline junction switch relative to the reversing connection at least two trips around most of the main line must intervene between the "out" and the "back," ensuring a journey of at least moderately respectable length.

HOW CLOSE TO THE PROTOTYPE CAN WE GET?

Literal interpretation of any extended segment of the trackage or operating pattern of the real RGS is out of the question in this modest area, so the station names copied or adapted can

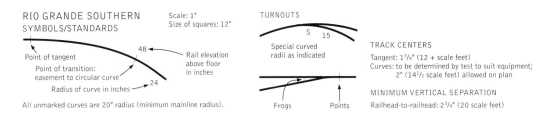

RIO GRANDE SOUTHERN
SYMBOLS/STANDARDS

Scale: 1"
Size of squares: 12"

Point of tangent
Point of transition:
easement to circular curve
Radius of curve in inches — 24
48 — Rail elevation
above floor
in inches

All unmarked curves are 20" radius (minimum mainline radius).

TURNOUTS

S
15

Special curved
radii as indicated

Frogs   Points

TRACK CENTERS

Tangent: 1³/₄" (12 + scale feet)
Curves: to be determined by test to suit equipment;
2" (14¹/₂ scale feet) allowed on plan

MINIMUM VERTICAL SEPARATION

Railhead-to-railhead: 2³/₄" (20 scale feet)

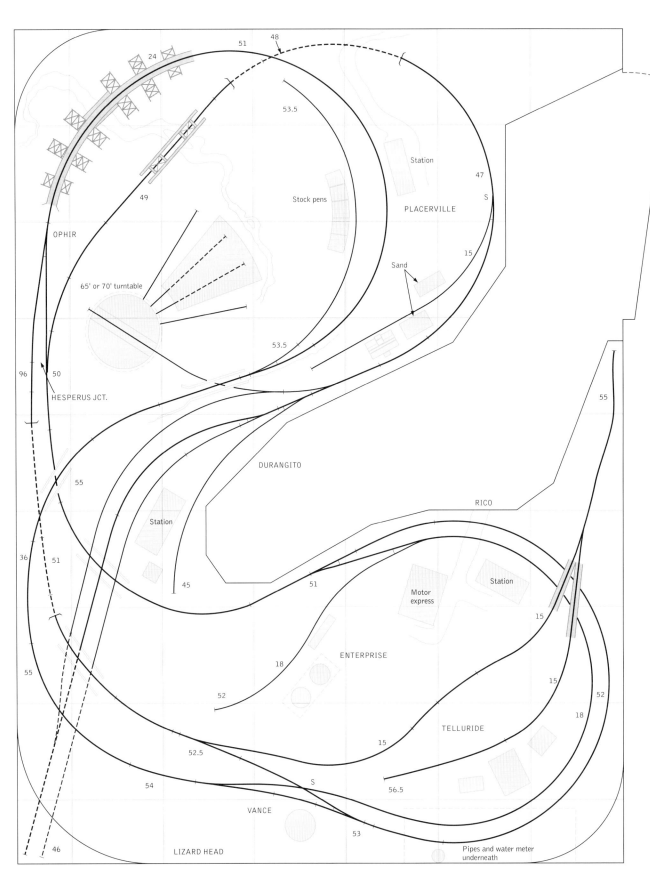

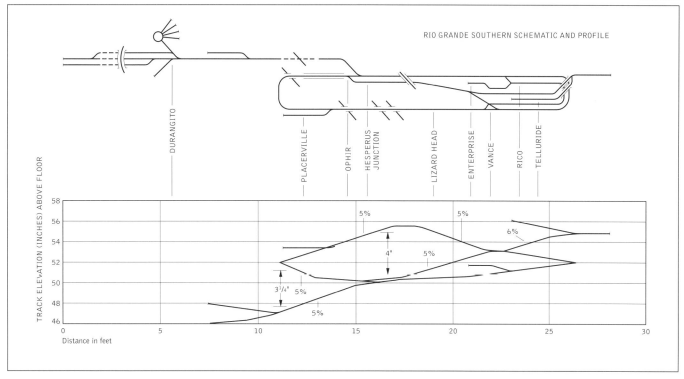

RIO GRANDE SOUTHERN SCHEMATIC AND PROFILE

Top: Tucked onto rock ledges and towering trestles, the Rio Grande Southern offered a perfect prototype for a model railroad which must make the most of the vertical dimension.

provide only the flavor of its operation.

On the other hand, there is room for individual buildings and structures of only moderately compressed scale, and the rugged terrain used to separate the scenes is thoroughly appropriate. Note that the watercourse emerging unseen behind the Durangito enginehouse flows away from the observer while dropping rapidly (the reverse of the situation with about 99 percent of the streams seen on model railroads). This allows the Ophir trestle to soar almost a hundred scale feet above its gulch without looking unnecessary.

On the backdrop there's nothing to stop us from using a direct copy of the real scene, so we can have famed Lizard Head itself (perhaps even partly in 3-D!) on the distant horizon without having to cover up any of our precious track with snowsheds (as the RGS did).

The Trans-Rockies Central Railroad

An HO layout pushed through, behind, and around

formidable obstacles, and designed for

territorial expansion as more space become available

THE TRANS-ROCKIES Central, a free-lance railroad of the late-steam era set in mountainous Canadian Pacific/Great Northern/Northern Pacific territory, is planned from the beginning for two distinct stages of construction. Initially, enough space in the basement family room is to be held off limits to railroading to serve as a play area for the younger members and to accommodate some of their bulkier gear. In due course, the railroad can push into this territory and even go on to the challenges of penetrating the utility area beyond.

THE FIRST STAGE – AND FIRST OBSTACLES

Intended to provide some mainline running along with full operation of the pike's major yard, the 14 x 15-foot first stage is essentially a dogbone with the two sides of its shank treated as separate portions of a single-track main line. Experience in overcoming obstacles which will come in handy later is to be acquired in fitting several tracks through a paneled enclosure hiding the squatty water heater and the overhead gas meter and regulator; between them they determine the height of the railroad.

Calgary is a separate station, schematically quite a distance from the division-point yards at Broken Bow, so it is raised 3" (22 scale feet) above its neighbor. A stretch of retaining wall emphasizes the separation without taking up any space.

In anticipation of second-stage construction, a turnout that for the time being goes nowhere is shown over the gas regulator in the lower right corner. Its points are far enough removed from the paneling above it to permit any troubleshooting that might be necessary during operation of the completed railroad, but the switch would be a stinker

── *Author's Insight* ──────────

The Trans-Rockies Central turns out to be an exercise in coping with a number of impediments common to many model railroad plans:
• For political reasons, occupancy of much of the basement area must be deferred until the passage of time has reduced family occupancy requirements; smart planning for worthwhile interim operation with a minimum of temporary trackage is in order.
• Obstacles aplenty there are, establishing both minimum and maximum track heights at various points, to the extent that one end of any practical main line must be so much higher than the other that a continuous-run connection is impractical.

Mitigating these problems is a matter of making use of all the tricks in the book. As a free-lance line, the T-R can assume its so nondependent on open-top mineral traffic that loop-to-loop operation of passenger and closed-top freight consists only will do.

The purposely vague route in the western provinces, borrowing terrain and place names from anywhere with mountains—Maryland, Austria, Montana—is limited to conventional (24" radius in HO) curve standards, with room allowed for easements.

to install during the repitching and reconnecting process that will precede the opening of the pike's "Eastern Extension" through the Rockies.

MORE OBSTACLES

Engineering a practical path through the toils of the furnace-chimney connection while starting from the level dictated by the gas appliances and leaving acceptable access for opening windows occasionally is at least as severe a challenge as that faced by the Canadian Pacific in Kicking Horse Pass. The answer is the same—two spiral tunnels. With them, the grade on the Big Hill is kept to 3.5 percent, which is a good model representation of the prototype's 2.2 percent so far as justifying helper engines and providing impressively vertical scenery is concerned. The deep

scene extending back more than four feet from a "viewing notch" between Nimrod and Blaser will be impressive; the beneath-mountain access from the rear makes it practical.

Curves are necessarily limited to conventional standards (24") at many points on the main line. This will cause no operating problems for the 2-8-8-2s which the Trans-Rockies will use to conquer the grades, but the matter of clearance between tracks has to be considered when that boiler front swings out into space. Tests before the track goes down are essential; from an appearance standpoint, as little widening as is necessary to let the full-length passenger cars clear the articulated's running boards on the passing tracks is desirable. Cutting it too close would be worse, because the S-curved route

A Canadian Pacific passenger train in the Fraser River Canyon in British Columbia.

won't always allow the dispatcher to keep the 2-8-8-2s on the outside track all the way.

A BIT OF BACKTRACKING

As is typical for a railroad of this size where the emphasis is on mainline operations with fairly long runs, walk-around access is provided to all points. It is necessary to backtrack a bit at one point (between Zap and Calgary) to follow a train over the entire route, and this means that the generally desirable situation of always having west to the left, east to the right as you face any segment of main line cannot be maintained.

We have chosen to have the most important sections of line (those through

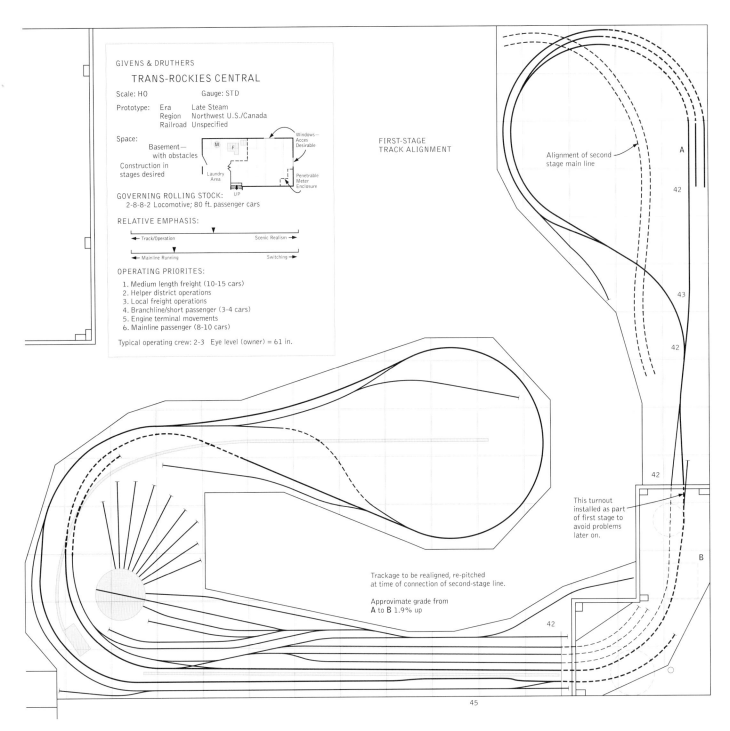

GIVENS & DRUTHERS

TRANS-ROCKIES CENTRAL

Scale: HO   Gauge: STD

Prototype: Era   Late Steam
            Region   Northwest U.S./Canada
            Railroad Unspecified

Space:
       Basement—
          with obstacles
    Construction in
    stages desired

GOVERNING ROLLING STOCK:
  2-8-8-2 Locomotive; 80 ft. passenger cars

RELATIVE EMPHASIS:

← Track/Operation   Scenic Realism →

← Mainline Running   Switching →

OPERATING PRIORITES:

1. Medium length freight (10-15 cars)
2. Helper district operations
3. Local freight operations
4. Branchline/short passenger (3-4 cars)
5. Engine terminal movements
6. Mainline passenger (8-10 cars)

Typical operating crew: 2-3   Eye level (owner) = 61 in.

M   F

Windows—
Acces
Desirable

Laundry
Area

Penetrable
Meter
Enclosure

UP

FIRST-STAGE
TRACK ALIGNMENT

Alignment of second
stage main line

A

42

43

42

42

This turnout
installed as part
of first stage to
avoid problems
later on.

B

Trackage to be realigned, re-pitched
at time of connection of second-stage line.

Approximate grade from
A to B 1.9% up

42

45

Broken Bow and on east through Zap) follow the rule. Once you get in the Spiral Tunnel territory—as you are particularly aware if you've tried to orient yourself there in the Canadian Rockies as a train works its way through the maze—things are going to be so confusing that whether the train is heading east or west doesn't matter!

THE LAKE PATRICIA BRANCH

Yet a third stage of construction is provided by the Lake Patricia branch, a passenger-oriented spur taking Pull-man passengers from the East directly to their resort. Since this line is hooked on backwards so far as the principal direction of traffic flow is concerned, the operating department will have to consider several options in handling the through passenger cars, all of them interesting from a railfan standpoint even if they would be of varying degrees of attractiveness economically to a prototype railroad.

To make the best use of the space, this railroad has been designed to use no. 5 turnouts at most points, which means they will have to be built by hand if using commercially available prefabricated ones in other sizes. Considering the 24″ mainline curvature, no. 4½s (Atlas "no. 4s") would be a satisfactory substitute in most cases. At some points in the plan the space saving of curved turnouts is essential; fortunately, those shown are now commercially available.

Opposite: A freight train negotiating Tunnel no. 2 of CP's famed Spiral Tunnels in Kicking Horse Pass. The Trans-Rockies Central is to be a freelance railroad, but will draw heavily from Canadian Pacific's rugged crossing of the Rockies for its scenery.

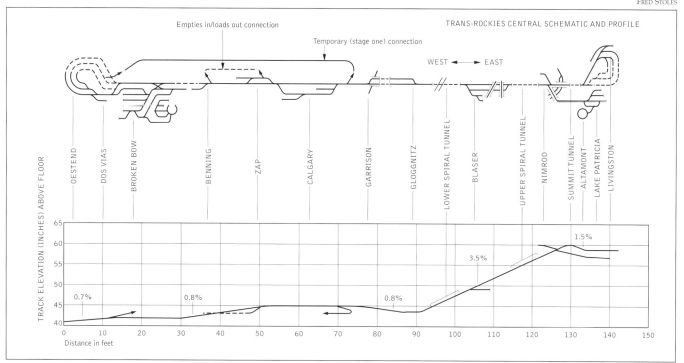

Empties in/loads out connection

Temporary (stage one) connection

TRANS-ROCKIES CENTRAL SCHEMATIC AND PROFILE

WEST ◄──► EAST

OESTEND
DOS VIAS
BROKEN BOW
BENNING
ZAP
CALGARY
GARRISON
GLOGGNITZ
LOWER SPIRAL TUNNEL
BLASER
UPPER SPIRAL TUNNEL
NIMROD
SUMMIT TUNNEL
ALTAMONT
LAKE PATRICIA
LIVINGSTON

TRACK ELEVATION (INCHES) ABOVE FLOOR

65
60
55
50
45
40

1.5%
3.5%
0.7%
0.8%
0.8%

0   10   20   30   40   50   60   70   80   90   100   110   120   130   140   150

Distance in feet

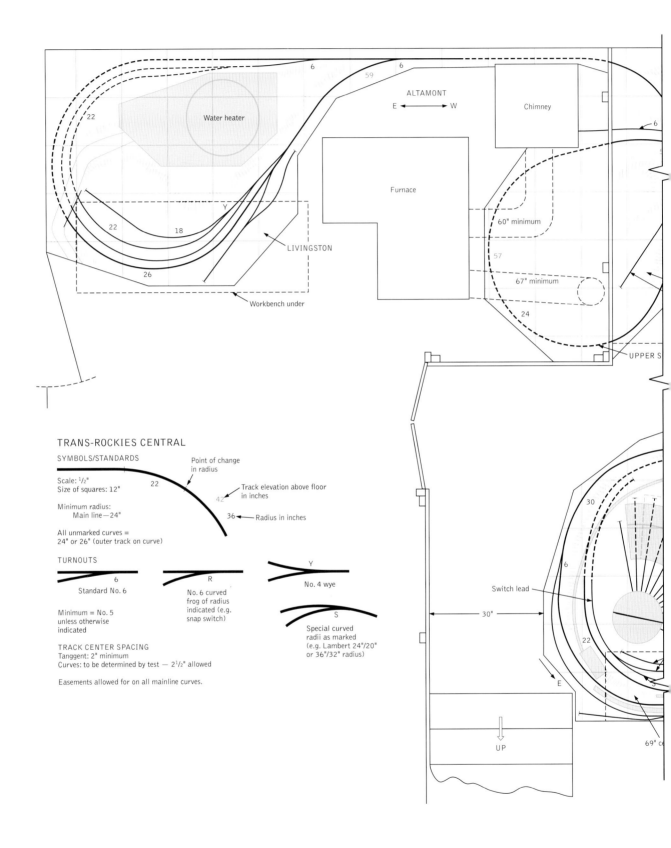

ALTAMONT

E ← → W

Water heater

6   6   6

59

22

22   18

26

Y

LIVINGSTON

Workbench under

Chimney

Furnace

60" minimum

57

67" minimum

24

UPPER S

TRANS-ROCKIES CENTRAL

SYMBOLS/STANDARDS

Point of change
in radius

22

Track elevation above floor
in inches

42

36 ← Radius in inches

Scale: ¹/₂"
Size of squares: 12"

Minimum radius:
    Main line—24"

All unmarked curves =
24" or 26" (outer track on curve)

TURNOUTS

6

Standard No. 6

R

No. 6 curved
frog of radius
indicated (e.g.
snap switch)

Y

No. 4 wye

S

Special curved
radii as marked
(e.g. Lambert 24"/20"
or 36"/32" radius)

Minimum = No. 5
unless otherwise
indicated

TRACK CENTER SPACING

Tanggent: 2" minimum
Curves: to be determined by test — 2¹/₂" allowed

Easements allowed for on all mainline curves.

30

6

Switch lead

30"

22

E

S

UP

69" c

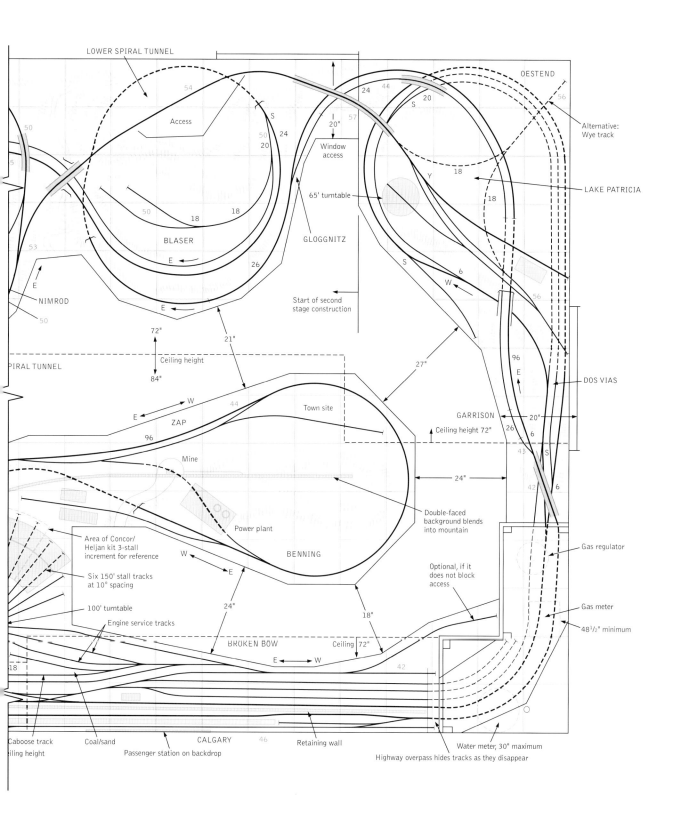

LOWER SPIRAL TUNNEL

54

OESTEND

50

Access

50 24

S

24 44

S 20

56

Alternative:
Wye track

20"

57

Window
access

18

65' turntable

Y

LAKE PATRICIA

18

50

18 18

BLASER

E

26

GLOGGNITZ

S

W 6

56

53

E

NIMROD

E

Start of second
stage construction

96

E

DOS VIAS

50

72"

21"

27"

20"

Ceiling height

E W 44

ZAP

Town site

GARRISON

26 20

84"

SPIRAL TUNNEL

96

Mine

Ceiling height 72"

6

43 S

42 6

24"

Area of Concor/
Heljan kit 3-stall
increment for reference

W

E

Power plant

BENNING

Double-faced
background blends
into mountain

Six 150' stall tracks
at 10° spacing

Optional, if it
does not block
access

Gas regulator

100' turntable

24"

18"

Gas meter

Engine service tracks

BROKEN BOW

Ceiling 72"

48¹⁄₂" minimum

18

E W

42

Caboose track
eiling height

Coal/sand

CALGARY 46

Retaining wall

Water meter, 30" maximum

Passenger station on backdrop

Highway overpass hides tracks as they disappear

The Delaware & Allegheny Railroad

Five scale miles of heavy-duty mainline railroading

in N scale, one scene at a time

SQUARE-WISE, this is the second largest track plan in this book—12½ squares long by 7½ squares wide, to be built in a 14 x 21½-foot obstruction-free area that can be completely devoted to railroad. With over 100 turnouts, it's also among the most complex. Thanks to the compactness of N scale, the whole thing fits in one end of a 22-foot wide basement. And this pike concentrates on those things for which N is best noted: running long passenger and freight trains and accommodating hundreds of pieces of rolling stock, in and out of sight.

The theme of the Delaware and Allegheny is a heavy-duty, single-track, late steam era, mountain-crossing railroad like the Western Maryland or Clinchfield—but with the passenger traffic of the B&O's Chicago and St. Louis main lines combined. Why not—freedom to combine things that turn

you on and make the best "model prototypes" is the essence of model railroading!

SPIRAL AISLES; STRAIGHTER TRACK

It's a five-scale-mile trip from loop to loop of the D&A's main line, none of which overlaps itself thanks to the liberal use of double-faced backdrops. As is usually the case where the area is big enough to allow a choice, a spiral aisle arrangement works out somewhat better than a parallel-lobed one. There is a higher ratio of straight to curved track, and even though any railroad crossing the Alleghenies will have a lot of curves, the D&A should still try to get over the summit in straightforward fashion. Wrapping a railroad up to lit into a basement generally results in way too many horseshoes, so the spiral

(which in this case has about two complete circles less curvature than a back-and-forth arrangement would have) comes a little closer to reality.

Top priority for the D&A, though, is

Author's Insight

When a clear area, amounting to 80 or 100 square squares, is available, great possibilities—with some hazards—open up. Without double-decking, a single-track, once-through-each-scene, walkalong main line several scale miles long, with enough passing tracks to keep train crews and dispatcher alert, is feasible. A mountain-crossing route can include both slopes, making practical a continuous-run connection allowing heavy traffic in open-top cars to move in proper empty/load directions.

The N gauge Delaware & Allegheny plan addresses two big layout hazards. To maintain morale in an at-best lengthy proj-

ect, an interim connection provides early loop-to-loop operation.

With an eastbound grade so steep that passenger and freight helper service is for real, on occasions it would be nice to circulate impressive consists without that complication. An asymmetrically gentler westbound grade allows just that.

Filling most of the central area, a spiral peninsula provides relatively long straightaways while requiring only one space-eating blob, illustrating the efficiency of this particular design approach.

Behind the roundhouse a hinged drop-down pond can provide access minus a "hold this hatch cover for me, will ya" plea.

passenger train switching. This is respected by envisioning Confluence City as pretty much the counterpart of the B&O's Cumberland, Maryland, where the two lines from different western terminals come together. D&As traffic isn't quite heavy enough to justify running separate trains through to the east, though, so its operating pattern typically consists of combining trains on the way east and splitting them on the way back. With set-out diners, sleepers, and head-end cars to be shuffled, the double slip switches at both ends of the long platform tracks will be kept busy.

YARD AND SERVICE FACILITIES

While the station tracks are curved, both for appearance and to allow the freight and passenger areas of the terminal to share the spotlight by being located end-to-end rather than side-by-side, trackage at the ends of the platforms where coupling and uncoupling must take place is straight. The coach and head-end car yard ladder is also straight so a minimum of storage space will be lost in locating uncoupling ramps to work reliably under the long cars.

The D&A is accommodating itself to the diesel by building separate facilities at the west end of the Confluence City yards, leaving the steam engine terminal out front where the railfans can get a good look at its still-busy components.

Working in empties-in/loads-out arrangements for simulating open-top traffic patterns without having to actu-

The Delaware & Allegheny is a big railroad, big enough to feature one-scene-at-a-time scenic treatment. Passenger action similar to the B&O's operations at Cumberland, Maryland, carries a high priority.

ally load and unload the cars is no problem on a pike this big—in addition to the usual coal, how about woodchip traffic in outsized hoppers or gondolas as well? Because there will still be a lot more coal traffic than can be accounted for by the mine and power plant in evidence on this segment of what is a far longer and busier railroad, the optional continuous-run connection to allow solid trains of minerals to run eastward and meet their westbound empty counterparts trip after trip is worth

71

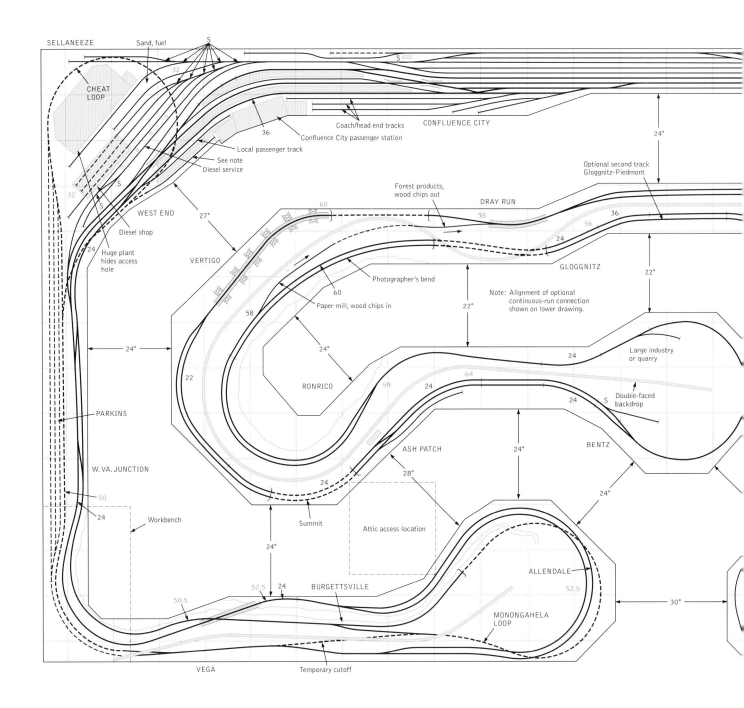

SELLANEEZE   Sand, fuel   S

CHEAT
LOOP
32

36

Coach/head end tracks   CONFLUENCE CITY
S   Confluence City passenger station
Local passenger track
See note
Diesel service

WEST END   27"   Forest products,   DRAY RUN
wood chips out   58
60   56   36
Diesel shop   24
Huge plant   GLOGGNITZ
hides access   VERTIGO   Optional second track
hole   Gloggnitz-Piedmont
24   58   60   22"
Photographer's bend
Paper mill, wood chips in   Note: Alignment of optional
continuous-run connection
58   shown on lower drawing.

24"   22"   Large industry
or quarry
22   24   Double-faced
RONRICO   59   24   backdrop
PARKINS   64   S
24   BENTZ
W. VA. JUNCTION   ASH PATCH   24"   24"
28"
50   24   24   24"
Workbench   Attic access location
ALLENDALE
Summit   52.5
52.5   24   BURGETTSVILLE   MONONGAHELA   30"
50.5   LOOP
24"
VEGA   Temporary cutoff

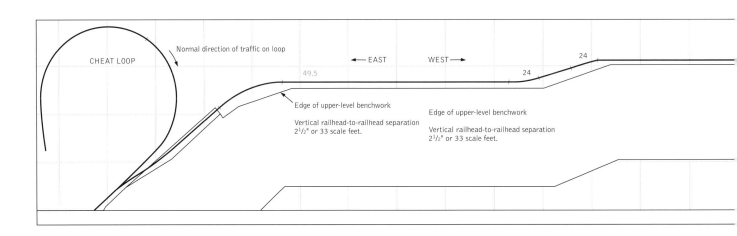

CHEAT LOOP   Normal direction of traffic on loop   ← EAST   WEST →   24

49.5   24
Edge of upper-level benchwork
Edge of upper-level benchwork
Vertical railhead-to-railhead separation
2¹/₂" or 33 scale feet.   Vertical railhead-to-railhead separation
2¹/₂" or 33 scale feet.

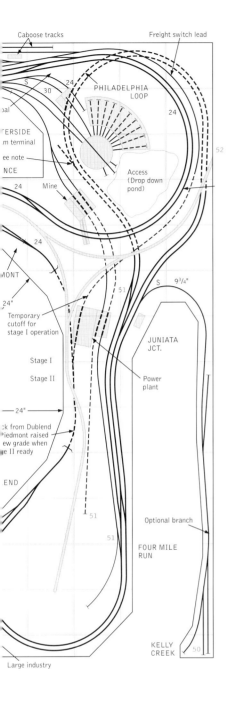

Caboose tracks

Freight switch lead

PHILADELPHIA LOOP

S

30

24

24

24

52

ERSIDE
m terminal

ee note

NCE

24

Mine

Access
(Drop down
pond)

MONT

24"

Temporary
cutoff for
stage I operation

51

S

9¾"

JUNIATA
JCT.

Stage I

Stage II

Power
plant

24"

ck from Dublend
iedmont raised
ew grade when
e II ready

51

END

51

Optional branch

51

FOUR MILE
RUN

KELLY
CREEK

50

Large industry

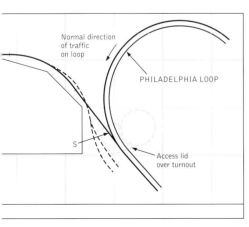

Normal direction
of traffic
on loop

PHILADELPHIA LOOP

S

Access lid
over turnout

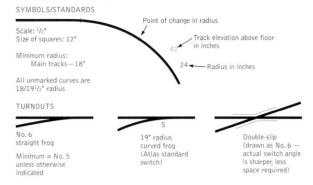

DELAWARE & ALLEGHENY

SYMBOLS/STANDARDS

Scale: ½"
Size of squares: 12"

Minimum radius:
Main tracks—18"

All unmarked curves are
18/19½" radius

Point of change in radius

Track elevation above floor
in inches

42

24 — Radius in inches

TURNOUTS

No. 6
straight frog

Minimum = No. 5
unless otherwise
indicated

S

19" radius
curved frog
(Atlas standard
switch)

Double-slip
(drawn as No. 6 —
actual switch angle
is sharper, less
space required)

TRACK CENTER SPACING

Tangent: 1¼" minimum — shown as 1⅓" (approximately)
Curves: shown as 1½" — actual spacing to be determined by test
or set at 1⅜" minimum

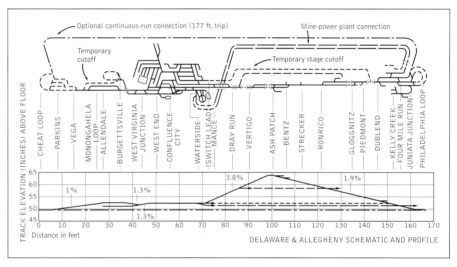

DELAWARE & ALLEGHENY SCHEMATIC AND PROFILE

considering. At 5.4 scale miles per circuit, these runs will keep a lot of rolling stock gainfully employed.

A SINGLE-TRACK GRADE

The D&A's Allegheny crossing is east of the junction between its Cheat and Monongahela lines, so traffic up its Ash Patch grade is dense; in fact, there would be ample justification (and, in N scale plenty of room) for double track all the way up and over. As drawn, the single-track bottleneck across Vertigo Trestle is the choice in the interest of making this bridge look even longer, higher, and more perilous than it would if double tracked, but a double/triple-track mountain crossing is still a good option.

As it is, we can't resist a segment of triple track from Four Mile Run to Juniata Junction for that big-time flavor. Bringing the five Philadelphia Loop switches out into the open is not only in the interest of comfort and reliability but also allows layover by the really long trains for which this pike will become noted.

At the other end of the railroad, Parkins provides layover capacity, though not nearly as much as could be useful. The slimness of N scale trains allows maintaining access to Parkins' turnouts by simply moving the top-level tracks through West Virginia Junction out toward the aisle and leaving them exposed from above, behind an embankment but in front of the backdrop.

OPTIONS

Also flexible is the location of the Ash Patch summit. For the same reasons discussed in connection with the Durango, Ophir, & Northern plan the grades have been made highly asymmetrical, but they could be equalized to make both directions pusher grades or even to make the westbound climb the tough one.

As befits a pike of this complexity, construction in stages has been provided for, with temporary connections allowing a lot of railroading action before commencing some of the more complex and space-clogging construction required to bring the grand design to completion.

Milwaukee Road in 4 x 8 Chunks

The Milwaukee Road's electrified route over St. Paul Pass

in the Bitter Root Mountains on its Rocky Mountain Division

is the subject of this scenically oriented plan

SPACE IS unlimited on paper, but in fairness to the 9 per cent of modelers who don't have unlimited space, this HO layout has the following crucial restrictions:

• It's to be built in sections no more than 4 feet wide and 8 feet long, not as a modular or portable pike, but so that it can be moved once or twice in a lifetime and be reconstructed without starting too close to scratch.

• For the same reason, it must be an island-type pike so that its shape is not totally dependent on the room it will occupy. The available area is about 12 x 16 feet, which must include working and viewing room around the railroad.

• There is a door (at lower right, fig. 1) inconsiderately located far enough from the corner of the room to foul the corner of our island pike, and it cannot be removed or rebuilt to swing out of instead of into the room.

• The minimum radius for some of the motive power is 22", although a 20" passing-track radius is acceptable.

The Milwaukee Road had two sections of electrification on its Pacific Extension, a 438-mile stretch from Harlowton, Montana, to Avery, Idaho, on the Rocky Mountain Division, and a 207 mile stretch between Othello and Tacoma, Washington, on its Coast Division. Both electrified and non-electrified trackage are to be represented on our layout so that we can operate steam, diesel, and electric locomotives. This limits the locale to the Harlowton,

Avery, or Othello areas where one form of motive power was exchanged for another during the era of juice operation. We'll settle on Avery, which puts us in the scenic Bitter Root Mountains.

Author's Insight

What has to be out of scale in even the most spacious layouts? The curves! *Accurately* modeling the Pennsy over its Allegheny summit would mean accommodating a minimum HO radius of 84". The name of the game in vignette modeling is *control of viewpoints*.

The out-of-scale curves needed to stay within the room or basement are kept out of sight; within the featured scene or scenes, visible curves are of gentleness appropriate for the location depicted—introduced "cosmetic" bends so proportioned that trains look gorgeously natural rounding them.

This example of a Milwaukee Road HO pike in a 12 x 16-foot space is constricted to an island design in 4 x 8 segments in the interest of adaptability to reassembly in future homes of unpredictable configuration. Given the resulting compact area, the choice of locale is inevitable—Avery, Idaho, where steam or diesel and electric locomotives are exchanged at the foot of the twisty, arduous climb to the summit of the Bitter Roots. There's room for a long stretch of cosmetic-curve radius on each side of such a plan—in this example, one in the Avery yard, the other featuring a towering trestle. A double-faced backdrop and "viewing notches" enforce one-scene-at-a-time railfanning.

The brick substation in the background dominates the lonely division point of Avery, Idaho.

How do we go about determining the basic track-plan concept? Well, the constraints of the 4 x 8-foot sections and the required 24″ aisle space on the free sides of the layout pretty well determine the shape of the basic space. We can squirm some, but it's going to look about like A in fig. 1. The normal approach to providing two sweeping cosmetic curves in this space would be to lay out a very gently squeezed dogbone (B in fig. 1), but it doesn't seem to fit very well here. Also, we're committed to having a division-point yard with fairly long tracks—those big electrics should have reasonably long trains to haul—so it looks as if one of our possible vignette areas will be occupied more by yard trackage than by a slender right of way curving through unspoiled wilderness.

Later steps in our preliminary doodling (C and D in fig. 1) indicate that a convex yard would be best, that some slightly unconventional trackwork is needed to accommodate one of those towering steel trestles so typical of Milwaukee's extension to Puget Sound, and that there will have to be a lot of hidden track if we're going to have steam and electric power operated properly in their respective territories.

What emerges from our doodlings? A single-track main line with no passing tracks! The schematic, fig. 2, shows that the railroad will be an out-and-back operation (as it has to be if motive power types aren't to get scrambled) from the east and west ends of the Avery yard. It's a messy-looking affair at the left end of the plan view with those three layers of track crossing each other at what appear to be extremely awkward shallow angles. If we could view the plan in three dimensions from the side, we'd see a helix of track in this region. Hidden by the rugged Bitter Root topography, the helix lifts the main line an extra four inches, so vertical crowding is actually minimal. Helix construction cannot be considered a beginner's project, but it's not so complex that we should deny ourselves the advantage that the helix offers.

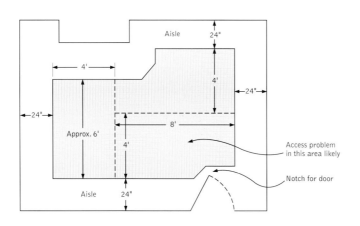

Aisle

24"

4'

4'

24"

24"

8'

Approx. 6'

4'

Aisle

24"

Access problem in this area likely

Notch for door

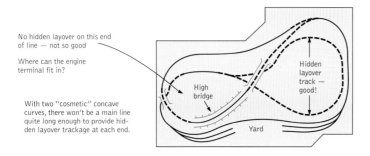

No hidden layover on this end of line — not so good

Where can the engine terminal fit in?

With two "cosmetic" concave curves, there won't be a main line quite long enough to provide hidden layover trackage at each end.

High bridge

Hidden layover track — good!

Yard

Blocking the aisle once is O.K.

Make the yard's cosmetic curve into a convex curve, and you can add another "lap" to make the main line long enough for two layover tracks. Now, how high can the bridge be?

W

Z

X

Y

Yard

W to X: 8' at 1% = 1"
X to Y: 16' at 1/2% = 1"
Y to Z: 18' at 3% = 6½"
Total elevation: 8½"

8½" is 60' in HO — not a very high bridge

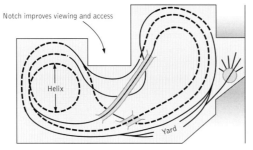

Notch improves viewing and access

Helix

Yard

Solution: add a one- or two-turn helix as part of the ascending trackage to the high-bridge loop. One 22"-radius helix adds 4½" (22 x 2π x .03) or 30' in HO. Thus, bridge can be 90-120 feet high — much more impressive.

Fig. 1

A train leaving Avery in either direction proceeds to one of the end loops and eventually returns to Avery, just as if its motive power had gone to the next division point (Harlowton on the east, Othello on the west) and returned on a different train. That 22″ minimum radius must fit into the 48″-wide sections, so there is no room for passing tracks anywhere except at the Avery yard. How can we run a single-track railroad without them? It's easy. The hidden parts of the two end loops are each long enough to hold two normal-length trains. If we wire the sections on the schematic labeled "Layover E-l," "Layover E-2," etc., as separate electrical blocks, the line will accommodate four or five trains at a time, with those that are theoretically on other divisions properly hidden during their layover (offstage) periods.

Milwaukee Road's line over the Bitter Roots doesn't actually loop over itself (à la Southern Pacific on Tehachapi in California or Canadian Pacific at Kicking Horse Pass in British Columbia), but it has enough curved, mountain-climbing track that it could readily do so without much change in its character. Figure 3 shows how we "improve on nature" twice to justify creating vignettes where we can see two trains moving at the same time. This is accomplished by having one of the loops encompass the point at which the eastward ruling grade along the St. Joe River changes from 0.3 to 1.71 per cent. This point, of course, becomes Avery, where steam or diesel motive power adequate for the flatlands is swapped for the mighty combinations of electric road and helper power needed to lift transcontinental tonnage over the divides. Now we can watch, for example, a westbound steam- or diesel-powered train roll "off the mountain" on the lowest level while eastbound electrics grind uphill nearby with another train that has completed its engine and crew change at the division point.

DETAILS, DETAILS!

In any pike where you're trying to squeeze in the most operating and scenic realism, the details of the track design, and the scenic features that will hide the crowding become particularly important. Even if you have the room to spread the same plan out into more generous proportions, you can use some of

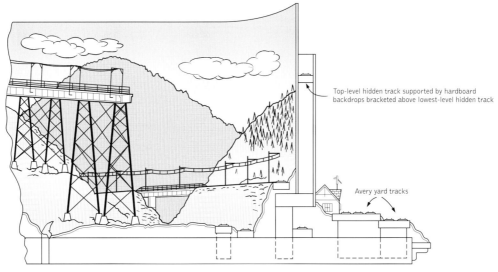

Top-level hidden track supported by hardboard backdrops bracketed above lowest-level hidden track

Avery yard tracks

CROSS SECTION A-A

the tricks of minimum-area track planning to improve the railroad. If you do have more space, you then have a choice: You can maintain the same tight design and construction of our Milwaukee Road plan and add features such as a passing track or an additional layover siding, or you can use the extra room to avoid such space-saving but extra-effort features as curved turnouts.

As shown in the plan, our Milwaukee pike leans heavily on curved turnouts. Except for a few in the yard, every turnout on the railroad either must be or should be curved to provide the best in operation and appearance. Fortunately, prefab curved or curvable turnouts fitting many of these situations are now available in HO. Also on the plus side, the number of turnouts is modest for a pike of this size and ambition, and they are accessible even where they're out of sight.

To achieve greater difference in elevation between electrified and non-electrified divisions, Avery yard is on a slight slope, but not more than 0.5 percent lest we create an unintentional hump yard. The slope also keeps the foreground storage tracks and the engine terminal leads somewhat below the main line and its station and passing tracks so we can see and appreciate the majestic sweep of the *Olympian Hiawatha* or no. 263 (the transcontinental fast freight) on the main line's big cosmetic curve. The difference in elevation isn't much—at most, half the height of a train—but it makes a big difference in how well the mainliners show up.

Our old friend the double-faced

backdrop shows up in doubly utilitarian form. Not only does it visually separate the two halves of the railroad, but as the cross-section shows, it supports and conceals a vital segment of the upper layover loop. This rather daring stunt will be extra-tricky if your electrified territory is actually operated by catenary. Well, as we agreed, this isn't a beginner's Christmas-tree outfit. Fortunately, there should be very few derailments on such a generous curve. A train which has successfully pulled and pushed its way to the summit via the 3 per cent grades is not likely to get in trouble up here.

On the opposite side of the railroad we have our other vignette areas, but at a glance it certainly doesn't look as if we've lived up to those brave ideals we established back at the start of this chapter. The Falcon trestle towers impressively over the tracks below (it's over 100 scale feet above the pond) on a generous radius, and it can be built to the distinctly Milwaukee Road design (diagonal bracing only). On the lower tracks, however, we've reverted to strictly model railroad curvature standards. Doesn't that ruin the whole effect?

Not necessarily! Note that trains running on these tracks can only be seen from viewpoint B at the alcove near the foot of the high bridge, placing the viewer at the approximate center of those curves on the lower track levels. Under these conditions it's nearly impossible to judge the radius of a curve without secondary clues such as the size of known objects along the rim.

True, we know how long our cars and trains are, but even so, the illusion persists that the curve is far less sharp than it actually is. You can confirm this by setting up a train near eye level on curves of different radius (no track needed) and gazing at it from the center. So, by controlling the viewpoint and blanking out the scenes at the ends of the arc, we have gone a long way toward achieving prototypical appearance without departing from functional curve standards.

The effect is lost if the viewpoint is not close to the bottom track level, so we want to enforce some control in that direction, too. There's room in the alcove for a chair, and from a seated position the eyeballs of the spectator or operator are brought into the proper alignment. The yard side is operated while standing; with the big curves on that side we can accept the higher viewpoint scenically, and the standing posture is appropriate for looking across several secondary tracks to the main line.

A single fixed control location won't do for a two-sided layout. Fortunately, the whole railroad is small enough that a tethered control unit on a 10-foot cable anchored at the left end of the layout will take care of viewpoints B, C, and D as well as operations in the yard. The engine terminal deserves its own panel, though.

ADDITIONAL FEATURES

Additional features can and should be worked into the master plan. As is, the pike is not suitable for the local

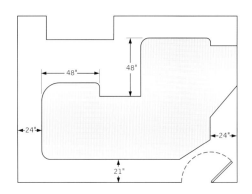

MILWAUKEE ROAD THROUGH THE BITTER ROOTS

Layout designed for HO scale
Scale of track plan: 1" = 1 foot
Overall layout size: 8' x 3' x 14'0"
Elevation above base level of layout shown thus: 0.0"
Electrified tracks:

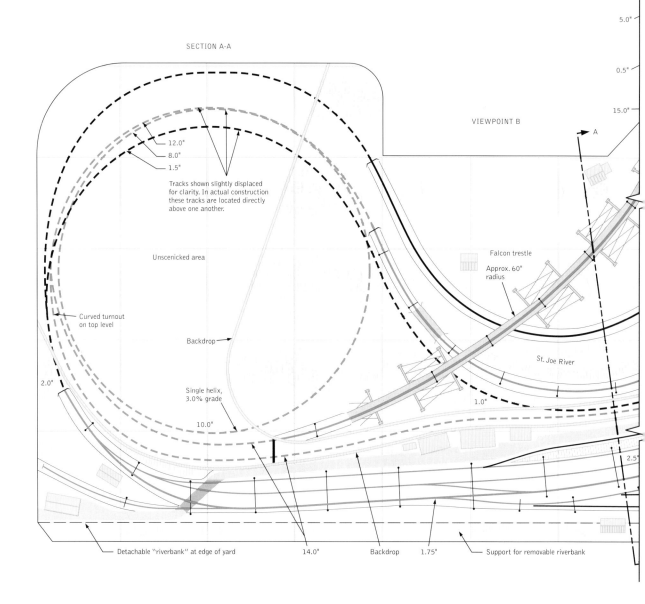

SECTION A-A

VIEWPOINT B

5.0"

0.5"

15.0"

A

12.0"
8.0"
1.5"

Tracks shown slightly displaced
for clarity. In actual construction
these tracks are located directly
above one another.

Falcon trestle

Approx. 60"
radius

Unscenicked area

St. Joe River

Curved turnout
on top level

Backdrop

2.0"

1.0"

Single helix,
3.0% grade

10.0"

2.5"

Detachable "riverbank" at edge of yard   14.0"   Backdrop   1.75"   Support for removable riverbank

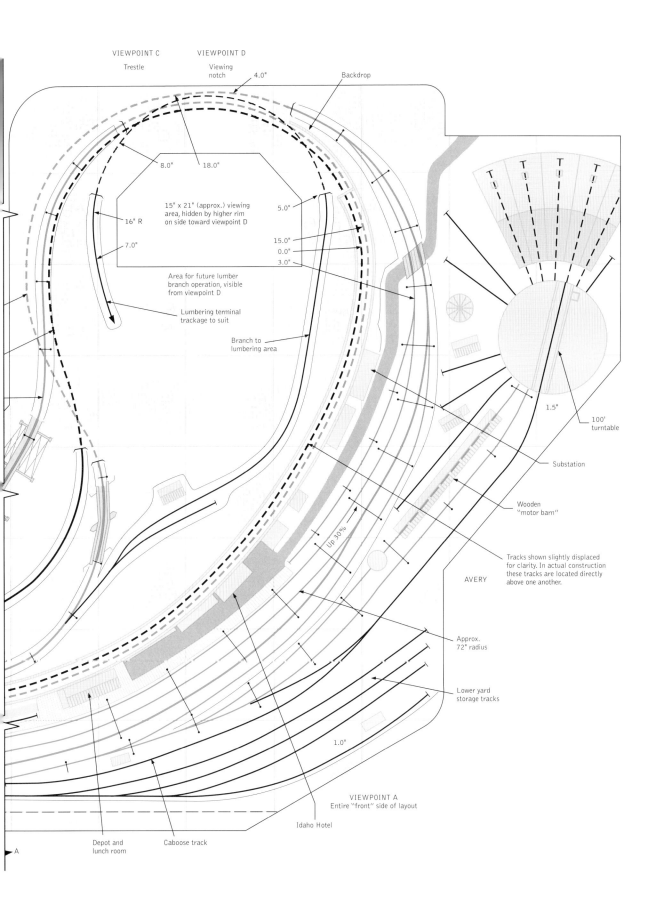

VIEWPOINT C
Trestle

VIEWPOINT D
Viewing
notch

4.0"

Backdrop

8.0" 18.0"

16" R

7.0"

5.0"

15.0"
0.0"
3.0"

15" x 21" (approx.) viewing
area, hidden by higher rim
on side toward viewpoint D

Area for future lumber
branch operation, visible
from viewpoint D

Lumbering terminal
trackage to suit

Branch to
lumbering area

1.5"

100'
turntable

Substation

Wooden
"motor barn"

Tracks shown slightly displaced
for clarity. In actual construction
these tracks are located directly
above one another.

AVERY

Up 30%

Approx.
72" radius

Lower yard
storage tracks

1.0"

VIEWPOINT A
Entire "front" side of layout

Idaho Hotel

Depot and
lunch room

Caboose track

A

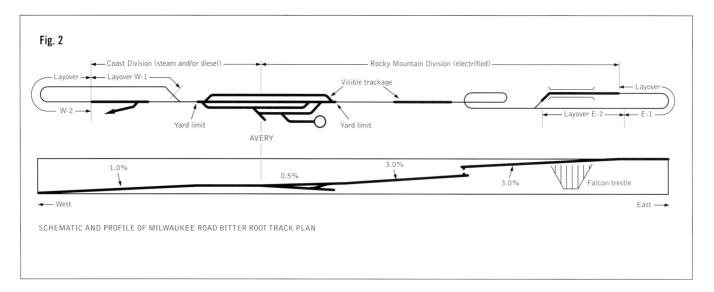

Fig. 2

SCHEMATIC AND PROFILE OF MILWAUKEE ROAD BITTER ROOT TRACK PLAN

freight devotee, nor is the prototype which is built through sparsely settled country possessed of few industries. But there's nothing to stop you from adding a lumber branch, and Avery yard provides enough switching activity in the model (probably more than in the prototype) to maintain operating interest.

Viewpoints C and D are essentially notches in the scenery and are designed to control the viewing angle without actually putting a frame around the scene. They're pretty high, so consider including a semi-permanent step (perhaps a fold-up attached to the underpinnings of the benchwork) for shorter viewers.

The extra sense of realism you get peering through one of these defiles, with all extraneous sights filtered out by forested mountain walls, has to be seen to be appreciated. As the scenery takes shape, other vantage points will suggest themselves, and if you're contouring the mountains on an as-you-go basis rather than building strictly to plan, you can adjust the terrain and foliage to take advantage of these little flashes of insight. For example, the scene looking down into the engine terminal from a point just to the left of viewpoint D also would likely be a winner.

In a plan as compact as this one, it's inevitable that some tracks are going to hang on the edge of the benchwork, as is the case at Avery. Here, a removable riverbank a few inches wide representing the St. Joe River greatly improves the scene without affecting the portability of the pike in the event of a move. Rules are made to be bent a little, now and then.

VARIETY IN ROLLING STOCK AND OPERATION

Variety is a keynote if the Milwaukee is our prototype. Every class of electric road locomotive that the railroad owned was operated over the Rocky Mountain Division electrification at one time or another. Even the EP-2 bipolars, built for the Coast Division electrification west of Othello, moved east in their twilight years to pull the *Olympian Hi* over the Bitter Roots. The 2-D+D-2 "Little Joes", diverted from their original Russian destination by the Cold War, wrapped up electric operation in 1974 along with the last of the EF-I boxcabs, which were as much as 49 years from their original outshopping dates! A train pulled by Joes M.U.'ed with diesels and pushed by a pair of boxcabs is legitimate, so there's not much you can't do in displaying your roster in action.

We can run time backwards, too. Build the railroad first as an all-diesel operation (with some overhead on the underside of the helix where it would be somewhat worse than difficult to install it later), then erect the Milwaukee's classic wooden-pole catenary in the next phase, and end up by resurrecting steam "west" of Avery when the roundhouse is finished.

Not a Milwaukee fan, nor inspired by the novelty of electrified operation in North America? No problem. The general format of this plan can be used to depict any mountain-climbing railroad at the point where its ruling grade changes abruptly. So, the pike could be the Maine Central in the White Mountains of New Hampshire, the Canadian Pacific at Kicking Horse Pass, the

Southern Pacific in the Cascade Mountains of Oregon, or any one of many other routes.

REVISIONS FOR OPEN-TOP TONNAGE.

In the Southeast, the Clinchfield's unbelievably tortuous but relatively gently graded crossing of the Appalachians could be the prototype. So could Soldier Summit on the Rio Grande in Utah, provided that an additional 15 or 20 per cent in layout length and width is available to allow for a double-track main line. There is one hitch: These lines carry a lot of tonnage (mainly coal) in open-top cars, and our loop-to-loop schematic would have the same loaded (or empty) cars traveling back and forth in both directions—great for conservation, but no real solution to the energy crunch unless you're willing to design a working hopper loading/unloading device and to use it between each trip or to provide room for a behind-the-scenes car swap. In such cases, the continuous-run mainline schematic is much to be preferred.

Figure 4 presents a concept for such revisions, the details of which are left as a mild challenge. There is a lot of hidden trackage, including a double-tracked helix and some three-tracked segments. Much of this is badly needed layover space for complete trains, however, so the overall track utilization is good. For really flexible operation, the crossover which is made possible by lengthening the helix into an oval is a real bargain in relation to the modest additional space required for it.

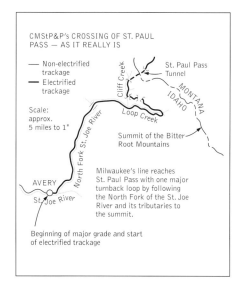

CMStP&P's CROSSING OF ST. PAUL PASS — AS IT REALLY IS

— Non-electrified trackage
— Electrified trackage

Scale: approx. 5 miles to 1"

St. Paul Pass Tunnel

Cliff Creek

Loop Creek

North Fork St. Joe River

MONTANA
IDAHO

Summit of the Bitter Root Mountains

AVERY

St. Joe River

Milwaukee's line reaches St. Paul Pass with one major turnback loop by following the North Fork of the St. Joe River and its tributaries to the summit.

Beginning of major grade and start of electrified trackage

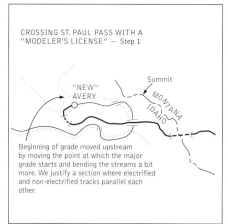

CROSSING ST. PAUL PASS WITH A "MODELER'S LICENSE" — Step 1

"NEW" AVERY

Summit

MONTANA
IDAHO

Beginning of grade moved upstream by moving the point at which the major grade starts and bending the streams a bit more. We justify a section where electrified and non-electrified tracks parallel each other.

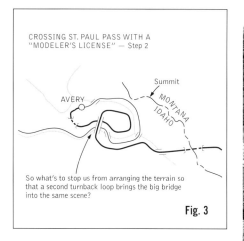

CROSSING ST. PAUL PASS WITH A "MODELER'S LICENSE" — Step 2

AVERY

Summit

MONTANA
IDAHO

So what's to stop us from arranging the terrain so that a second turnback loop brings the big bridge into the same scene?

Fig. 3

Not to scale — all visible curved track should be twice minimum radius or broader

Some hidden helix trackage shown displaced for clarity

— View block

Viewpoint (to see industry and part of main line)

High bridge

View point

Up

Access opening

Eastbound

Westbound

Down

To major industry

Eastbound

Westbound

Engine terminal area

Yard and station area

West (relatively steep grade)

East → (relatively moderate grade)

View point (to see track beyond access area through notch in scenery)

SCHEMATIC

Crossovers form layover track on main line

Hidden layover sections

Bridge

Major industry

Third track doubles as yard switching lead

Yard

Westbound

Eastbound →

Hidden layover sections

DOUBLE-TRACK CONTINUOUS-RUN VIGNETTE PIKE CONCEPT

Fig. 4

Milwaukee Road E-72 and E-79 descending Bitter Root Mountains near Falcon, Idaho.

PRR – Schuylkill Division

Layout design as influenced by a unifying theme

IF YOU *don't* plan things out thoroughly in advance, model railroading is fun! There are so many things to look at, to read up on, to try out for yourself, to have bull sessions about, to arrange in different combinations, to auction off or trade, and to rebuild that you'll never run out of enjoyable tidbits to savor.

If you *do* make thoughtful, well-integrated plans for your "empire," model railroading can be even more fun. If all the parts fit together into a consistent whole, you get double benefit from each thing you do because (1) each project is interesting in itself, and (2) the product of each project adds to the whole in a way that a scattershot approach cannot.

But doesn't restricting your choice of projects to only those that are within the scope of a one-man railroad eliminate a lot of fun possibilities? And won't planning everything ruin the opportunities of just going down to the layout room and doing what comes naturally of an evening? Not really. Even a small railroad involves so many wildly different operations—from research to carpentry to kit-building and weathering—that don't have to be done in any rigid sequence, that there's only an occasional need to do something that might not be your "first choice" project for the day.

Sticking to the general subject and era of your railroad does encourage you to get deeper into particular aspects of the hobby, though, and that's bound to pay off in a clearer understanding of just what steps and choices will lead to greater fun as the whole picture comes into focus.

Author's Insight

A fairly common set of "givens" and "druthers" matches a squarish area that, adjusting for the problem of entering the hobby area from the side, is in the range of 16 to 20 passenger-train-size square squares with a desire to model such a varnish-heavy railroad as the New Haven, New York Central, or even (gasp!) The Standard Railroad of the World.

Distilling as much of the flavor of the trackage and operations of such a railroad as possible into that area is a matter of selecting/inventing an area with complex traffic and then searching for ways to make it fit, maintaining passenger-car curve standards and adequate walkaround aisleway access.

In the Schuylkill Divison case, a suburban station/satellite yard locale on a double-track main expanding to a three-track section leading to a flying junction says unmistakably that this must be the Pennsy, somewhere near its Philadelphia hub. To wind in a long main line in the desired single-deck plan, there must be some backtracking in following a train and many curved turnouts are required.

Key to fitting in the complex operations typical of this southeastern Pennsylvania area is the fortunate fact that there's a lot of space alongside those space-eating mainline loops, usable by adjusting the curve radius to the rolling stock involved.

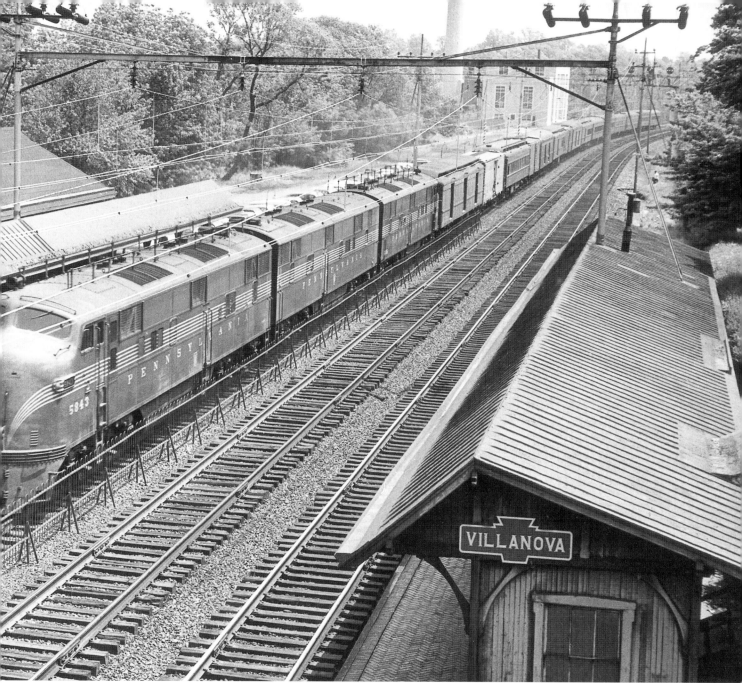

JACK EMERICK

YOU CAN STILL HANG LOOSE

Anyone who has been in the hobby for more than a few years will have a horror tale or two of fiascoes and near-misses in trying to second-guess the availability of particular models and supplies, with obvious gaps in the roster and a closet full of unbuilt kits to prove it. All you have to do is to finish scratchbuilding something tricky and distinctive, it seems, to induce some unheralded manufacturer to bring out an excellent fall-together kit of the same item. On the other hand, waiting for a well-advertised item which would be the key to your *Broadway Limited* or coal-mine branch can be equally frustrating when it shows up—five years late—out of scale and "behind scratch."

The defense? Plan your pike, based where possible on items already at hand, so that you have a fair number of alternatives at your disposal as work progresses. As it is, you'll have plenty to do just working with whatever models and supplies are available. If mass-produced ore cars become available instead of the coal hoppers that would have been your first choice, alter your plans for a power plant to that of a receiving end of a steel mill. You'll still have a busy main line serving an obviously important purpose and with a logical combination of hardware.

Caught in similar situations, a proto-type railroad will usually make do with what it has in its closet or otherwise adjust to the situation; e.g., hauling

The PRR track plan on pages 86-87 captures the flavor of Pennsy passenger routes radiating from Philadelphia. The multi-track mains, flanked by suburban depots such as this at Villanova, Pa., can host diesel, steam, and electric operations.

gravel trains with off-duty commuter 4-6-0s, or leasing diesels (often in spectacularly different paint schemes) from across the continent to cope with an unexpected traffic surge. There is some predictability to even the most improbable existence, though, so if you have a plan and move in its general direction every time you buy, swap, build, or modify, the result will still lead to a pike that makes the most of every square foot, dollar, and hour.

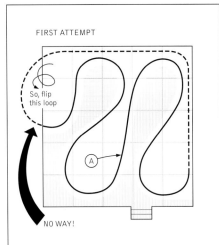

FIRST ATTEMPT

So, flip this loop

NO WAY!

Flipping the left turnback loop into a "half figure eight"
eases the whole situation and even allows space for
another aisle — the key to a workable scheme for final
development.

FINAL MAINLINE SCHEME

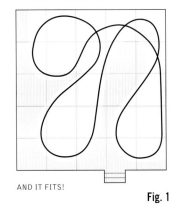

AND IT FITS!

Fig. 1

The total space allotted for the Schuylkill Division
is 26 x 27 feet, and minimum mainline radius will
be 54 inches. To make preliminary sketches of
basic track and aisle routing, we'll divide this
space into 25 five-foot track-planning squares.*
Figure an aisleway to be approximately a half
square (30 inches) wide.

The only place for the yard is on the central diagonal at A — the longest possible straightaway. A
three-lobed mainline route would represent a
good compromise between no-stoop accessibility
and length of run, but our first attempt shows that
it just won't fit.

* To arrive at a convenient size for a track-planning square, use the formula R + 2C, where R is
the minimum mainline radius and C is the suggested track-center spacing for that radius. For a
complete explanation of track-planning squares,
see Kalmbach's *Track Planning for Realistic
Operation*, by John Armstrong.

THE PASSENGER PENNSY —
IN A SQUARE

As an exercise in putting it all
together according to plan but with
stay-loose options, consider capturing
an adequate slice of Pennsylvania
Railroad passenger railroading within
the confines of a square layout area. No
need to worry about generating PRR's
family look; the erstwhile "Standard

Railroad of the World" maintained its
distinctive designs and practices so
thoroughly that even an Espee fan coming upon an unpainted model of a P70
day coach would have no trouble in
identifying it as Pennsy. The Pennsylvania ran millions of miles of its
"Blue Ribbon" services over Mid-
western flatlands on single-track mains,
but this PRR pike is to represent its
home-state, heartland territory of multi-

track main lines with a potential for
electrification, all in a context of rivers,
bridges, and hills.

Admittedly, passenger cars are not
exactly conducive to condensed railroading when you consider their 85-foot
length and the broad-radius curves they
require to let them flow by attractively.
Fortunately, we usually don't have to
condense passenger consists to the
degree that we do freights to accommo-

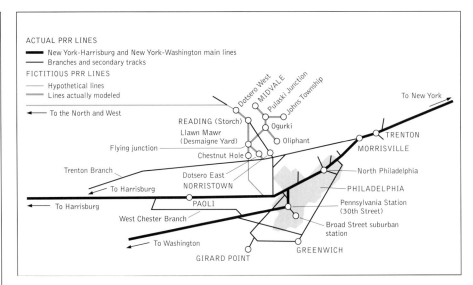

ACTUAL PRR LINES
— New York-Harrisburg and New York-Washington main lines
— Branches and secondary tracks
FICTITIOUS PRR LINES
— Hypothetical lines
— Lines actually modeled

← To the North and West

To New York →

Dotsero West
MIDVALE
Pulaski Junction
Johns Township
READING (Storch)
Ogurki
Llawn Mawr
(Desmaigne Yard)
Oliphant
Flying junction
Chestnut Hole
TRENTON
MORRISVILLE
Trenton Branch
Dotsero East
NORRISTOWN
North Philadelphia
← To Harrisburg
PHILADELPHIA
← To Harrisburg
PAOLI
Pennsylvania Station
(30th Street)
West Chester Branch
Broad Street suburban
station
← To Washington
GREENWICH
GIRARD POINT

Route on layout	Service or consist	Rationale*	Remarks
Main line (continuous route)	Through passenger	Philadelphia to north and west	Night train from New York
Main line (continuous route)	Local passenger	Trenton to anthracite country	Connections at Llawn Mawr
Main line (continuous route)	Mixed freight	New York (via Trenton) and Philadelphia to north and west	
Main line (continuous route)	Ore	Philadelphia import piers to north and west	Helper required
Main line (continuous route	Empty open-tops	New York and Philadelphia area to north	
Chestnut Hole to Llawn Mawr	Electric commuter	Philadelphia (suburban station) to end of electric district	M.U. equipment
Chestnut Hole to Storch	Locomotive-hauled commuter	Philadelphia (suburban station) to points beyond Llawn Mawr	Engine change to steam at Llawn Mawr
Chestnut Hole to westbound main (continuous route)	Mixed freight	New York to west via electrified route	Engine change to steam at Desmaigne Yard
Desmaigne to Ogurki	Coal empties, freight	Transfer run	May require a helper
Ogurki to Oliphant	Coal empties	Mine run	Coal co. Shay power
Johns Township to and Midvale	Mixed freight	Interplant traffic	One trip per day to from Desmaigne Yard

* Dignified term for "excuse for running"
Periodic layovers at Storch; engine change on trains from New York at Belle Paire

Fig. 2 The Schuylkill Division and its traffic patterns

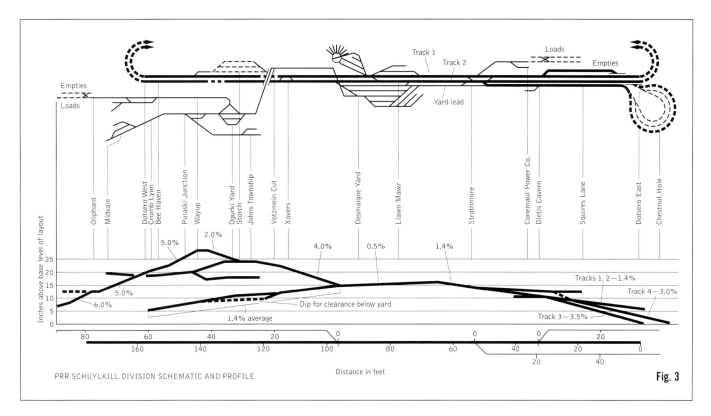

Empties
Loads

Track 1
Track 2

Yard lead

Loads
Empties

Oliphant	
Midvale	
Dotsero West	
Crumb Lynn	
Bee Haven	
Pulaski Junction	
Wayup	
Ogurki Yard	
Storch	
Johns Township	
Votzmein Cut	
Xovers	
Desmaigne Yard	
Llawn Mawr	
Strathmore	
Conemaul Power Co.	
Dietls Cavern	
Squires Lane	
Dotsero East	
Chestnut Hole	

Inches above base level of layout

5.0%   2.0%   4.0%   0.5%   1.4%

Tracks 1, 2 — 1.4%
Track 4 — 3.0%

5.0%
6.0%
Dip for clearance below yard
1.4% average
Track 3 — 3.5%

25
20
15
10
5
0

80   60   40   20   0   0   0   20
160   140   120   100   80   40   20   0
20   40

PRR SCHUYLKILL DIVISION SCHEMATIC AND PROFILE   Distance in feet   **Fig. 3**

date them on our layouts. Ordinarily, switching is the strong point of freight railroading, a facet of operation that's too good to pass by. So, in a pike that emphasizes the passenger train, we need to incorporate at least one point where trains originate and terminate or otherwise undergo consist changes: sleeper setouts, head-end switching, consolidation or splitting of trains from or for alternate lines. A big-city terminal can provide for all of these, of course, but its size will stunt the development of the rest of the track plan unless we're talking about a club-size pike. When it comes to providing the widest possible assortment of points of passenger operating interest, the New Haven, New York Central, Reading, and Jersey Central come to the fore. Their main and secondary lines in the densely populated Northeast formed a fascinating network. The Pennsy carried about the same number of passengers as all of them put together, and thus provides an even more lush selection of interesting points. So, let's see what can be done, and in O scale no less.

GETTING THERE BY DIFFERENT ROUTES

Full enjoyment of a large model railroad requires practical walkaround controls; enjoyable passenger-train switching means reliable automatic couplers; and space-gobbling items such as pas-

senger-radius, multi-track curves mean making the best use of every square foot. The timely success of some advanced developments may have to be taken on faith at the beginning, but the basic suitability and soundness of the track plan must be established (to scale!) before applying saw to lumber.

Like its prototype during its first hundred years of existence, this version of the Pennsylvania Railroad is not a temporary affair, but rather something to be built (at a reasonable pace) to endure. Its locale will be hilly, so we can be reasonably sure that wringing the most out of the space will mean multiple levels of track at some points. Thus, lowest-level trackage must be in perfect operating condition before being covered over in the later stages of construction. Nevertheless, the sequence of development is not something that has to be rigidly programmed. Whether final wiring and scenicking is to be done section-by-section or held until all basic trackage is completed can be left to your inclinations. If the H6sb gets built before the M1, yard wiring may get put ahead of wiring for the second main track. If the hopper-car project is accelerated along with the detailing and painting of the three-truck Shay, branchline priorities may rise accordingly. The important thing is that, ultimately, all the parts will complement each other, and that little time is frittered away on items that are

interesting but out of place (even with some stretch of the imagination) on your railroad.

It won't all fit, of course. No space, in any scale, is really adequate for modeling the more notable features of The Pennsylvania Railroad (take a reverent bow, please) to full scale. It's conceivable that PRR's Rockville Bridge (23 feet long in N scale) across the Susquehanna River near Harrisburg, Pa., or Horseshoe Curve (15 feet across in HO) near Altoona, Pa., can be fit in by sacrificing a lot of other things, but perhaps you really don't want to be confined to a single item, however magnificent. So, we're going to establish some priorities and use either selective compression on the survivors or design Pennsy-style fictionalized equivalents that will fit. Priority items are:

• Justification for a variety of passenger train consists and operations that include originating/terminating of trains, switching, engine changes.

• A main line that can accommodate any PRR passenger train without major restrictions from curvature or grade and yet emphasize good appearance in action.

• A major high-speed passenger-route junction that includes three- or four-track lines.

• Trackage that could be electrified, but electrification not to be mandatory to operation of complete layout.

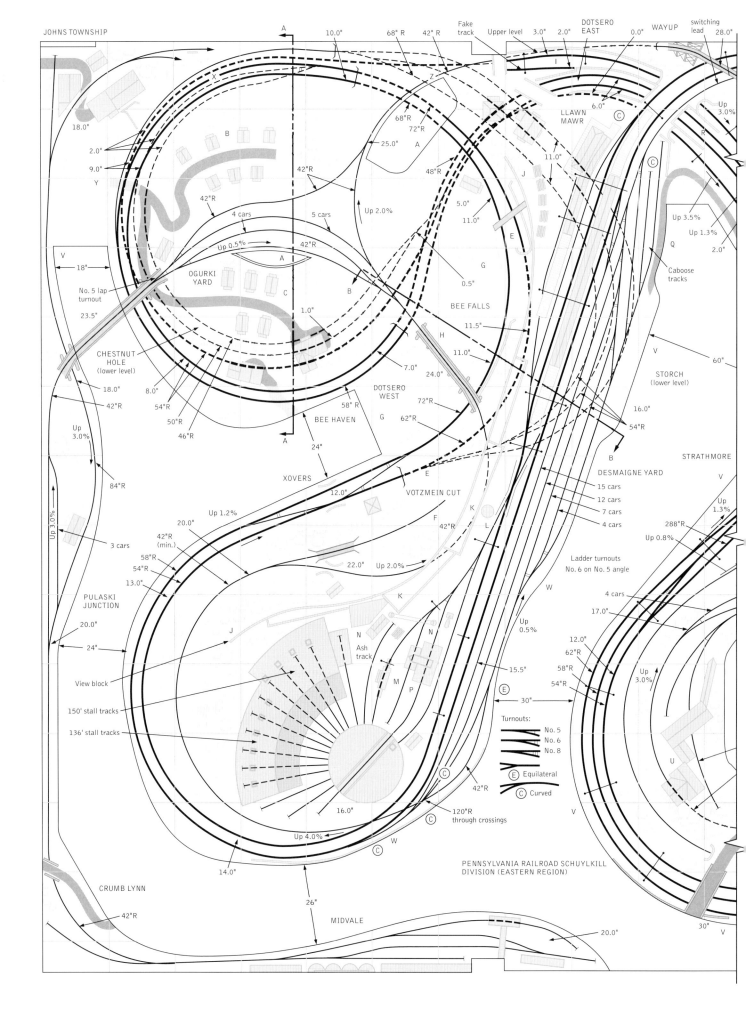

JOHNS TOWNSHIP

A

10.0"　68" R　42" R　Fake track　Upper level　3.0"　2.0"　DOTSERO EAST　0.0"　WAYUP　switching lead　28.0"

68"R
72"R
25.0"　A

18.0"

2.0"

9.0"

Y

42"R

42"R

4 cars

5 cars

V

18"

No. 5 lap turnout

23.5"

CHESTNUT HOLE
(lower level)

18.0"

42"R

8.0"

54"R

50"R

46"R

OGURKI YARD

Up 0.5"　42"R

A

B

C

1.0"

Up 2.0%

48"R

5.0"

11.0"

0.5"

7.0"

58" R

24.0"

DOTSERO WEST

BEE HAVEN

G

24"

XOVERS

B

H

11.5"

11.0"

72"R

62"R

BEE FALLS

LLAWN MAWR

6.0"

11.0"

J

E

G

Up 3.0%

Up 3.5%

Up 1.3%

2.0"

Q

Caboose tracks

V

60"

STORCH
(lower level)

16.0"

54"R

B

STRATHMORE

DESMAIGNE YARD

15 cars

12 cars

7 cars

4 cars

Up 3.0%

84"R

3 cars

Up 1.2%

20.0"

42"R
(min.)

58"R

54"R

13.0"

PULASKI JUNCTION

20.0"

24"

View block

150' stall tracks

136' stall tracks

J

E

VOTZMEIN CUT

12.0"

F

42"R

22.0"　Up 2.0%

K

K

L

N

Ash track

N

M

P

Ladder turnouts
No. 6 on No. 5 angle

W

Up 0.5%

15.5"

E

30"

288"R

Up 0.8%

4 cars

17.0"

12.0"

62"R

58"R

54"R

Up 1.3%

Up 3.0%

U

Turnouts:
No. 5
No. 6
No. 8
E Equilateral
C Curved

C

42"R

120"R
through crossings

16.0"

Up 4.0%

W

C

14.0"

CRUMB LYNN

42"R

26"

MIDVALE

PENNSYLVANIA RAILROAD SCHUYLKILL
DIVISION (EASTERN REGION)

V

30"

V

20.0"

Fake

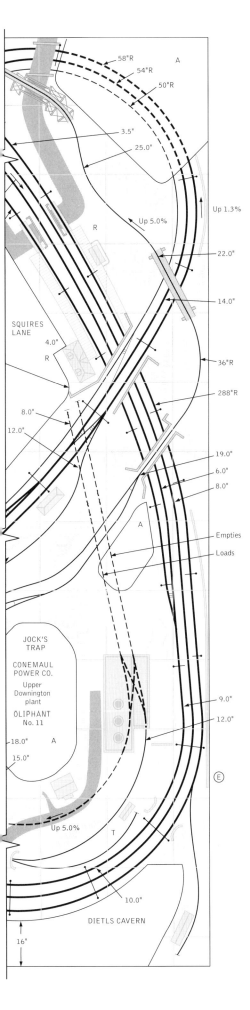

A Access and viewing points. Holes in scenery concealed from aisleways by height of topographic "lip" on side toward aisle

B Reduced-scale (to perhaps HO) miners' company town, visible only from a distance; view from Johns Township side blocked by terrain and trees

C Full-scale company-town houses in foreground below Ogurki Yard

D Company store

E Westbound main track in tunnel parallel to eastbound track on bank in this narrow section of Schuylkill Gorge

F "Abandoned" rock quarry spur with short trestle. Quarrying can be "resumed" when convenient

G Drop-leaf river protects bridge and prevents spectators from snooping beyond scenic bend; waterfall hides lower-level tracks

H Pin-connected Pratt deck truss

I Fake second track to complete illusion of flying junction. This track is visible only to those over 6'-11" tall and thus could be eliminated in final scenic treatment. Some of us still think it's a neat idea, though

J Ends of double-faced backdrop (height well above eye level) disappear into hill and foliage

K Rear side of mill and factory buildings

L Lally column disguised as tall factory standpipe, dissolving into the industrial mists somewhere above eye level

M Locomotive wash rack, limited electric locomotive inspection and servicing capability added with electrification. Ash pit and hoist

N Locomotive sand facilities

O Ten-stall roundhouse; depth (from turntable rim): 135'

P Coaling tower, 250 tons or larger. Alternate location (to space out points of interest) could be on main line in Xovers area

Q Steep, narrow driveway to caboose track area

R Suburban station buildings, platforms, and parking area (serving outer tracks only), Extensive PRR-style stone retaining walls in this area. Four tracks disappear into three portals in high fill supporting three upper-level tracks—pure Pennsy!

S Power plant absorbs loaded coal hoppers, returns empties. Condenser cooling—water pond provides excuse for compact installation with enclosed (presumably) car-dumper

T Spur for power-company switchers handling movements in and out of plant

U Coal mine complex, with trees, road, etc., conceals loads-out/empties-in connection immediately behind tipple. Careful, compact scenicking necessary to separate mine trackage from spur to power plant at lower level

V Flexible (made of cast rubber perhaps) embankment extends several inches below track and out into aisle but allows full-width use of aisle for passing railroaders and onlookers

W Workbench locations underneath railroad; ample headroom for seated work

X Curve, mill, retaining walls, etc., conspire to let three lower-level tracks disappear quietly under Johns Township runaround trackage

Y Optional drop-leaf pond surface to complete this peaceful pastoral industrial scene

Z Unscenicked or separately scenicked high-level track connecting Ogurki Yard and Oliphant Mine areas, 12" or more above next highest trackage

• Opportunities for PRR-style bridges, stone retaining walls, tunnel portals, and station platforms.

• Yard/layover/storage trackage for at least 25 passenger and 50 freight cars (modest numbers because the proprietor is a perfectionist and the acquisition, detailing, and completion of rolling stock to acceptable standards will be a slow process).

• Engine terminal facilities and operating requirements that justify the use of an unreasonably diverse spectrum of Pennsy steam: E6, K4, M1, maybe even D16 passenger power; M1b, I1, and even J1 freight locomotives; H6 or H9 and L1 branch or local-freight assignments; B6 and C1 yard engines; and someday maybe even a T1 and a Q2, the latter perhaps not completely rigid-frame!

• Harbor, riverside, or lineside heavy-industry scenic possibilities.

The space available is ideal in quality: an extra basement level beneath a large split-level home with finished walls, ample headroom, and no obstacles except for a single Lally column in the center of the 26 x 27-foot area. The biggest problem is quickly apparent: A square space always spells trouble when it comes to fitting in a long yet accessible main track. The same number of square feet in a two-to-one oblong space would yield a longer run and provide several straightaway sections where yards could be located. Our square space does have the advantage of making it easy to start track planning. As fig. 1 shows, there is only one place to locate the main yard, and it's also clear that this will be a continuous-run, double-track railroad. A square space of this size simply does not lend itself well to a point-to-point schematic in O scale, nor is the run of sufficient length to allow for passing tracks of adequate length for single-track operation.

Now, here's the key: Flip the third return-bend over (fig. 1 again) and you'll have a main line about a mile and a half long (in O scale) with excellent walk-in access. The Schuylkill Division plan is on its way. If the plan is to remain within bounds, there can only be one real engine terminal, one yard big enough to do some modest work on the consist of a mainline train, and one junction connecting multiple-track routes, so its locale should be at a point where all of these key items are close together. Even the PRR doesn't provide exactly this combination, so we'll gather scattered features of the real Pennsy for our Schuylkill Division and reassemble them in a setting reminiscent of the territory west and north of Philadelphia, not copying any one route or locality. There are elements of Paoli (outer terminus of electric commuter service), some flying junctions where double-track lines join without crossings, and minor subdivisional yards straddling main lines. Here, most traffic roars through, but some local trains terminate their runs.

THE TRAFFIC PATTERN

A traffic schematic of the Schuylkill Division (fig. 2), which shows how our imaginary lines fit into a real-world context, will help us to develop a track plan and appreciate the variety of traffic patterns that supplement the mainline parade of through trains. The flying junction in the vicinity of Squires Lane requires careful attention to grades so that the tracks cross over each other with proper clearance, and the network of branch lines also results in several separated crossings whose feasibility is best expressed on the profile diagram, fig. 3. There are a lot of close over/under clearances, some of which are possible only with fairly severe grades, but that is typical of eastern Pennsylvania PRR. We use some modeler's license to import a coal mine branch from some location that would be a little more westerly in the prototype state—the opportunity for secretly interchanging loads and empties at mine and power plant is too much to pass up.

There are many plausible train routings that can be simulated. Figure 2 lists enough to demonstrate that operations need never grow dull and repetitious on the Schuylkill Division, despite its basically round-and-round main line. On

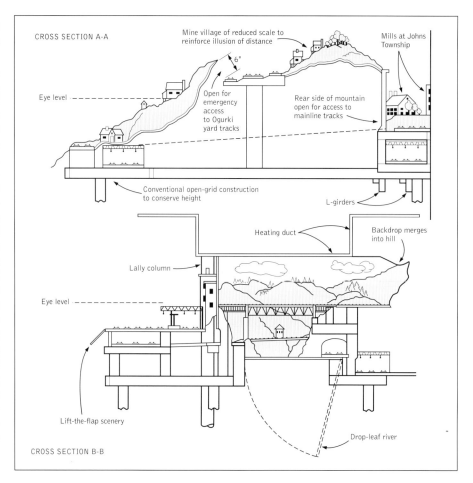

CROSS SECTION A-A

Mine village of reduced scale to reinforce illusion of distance

Mills at Johns Township

Eye level

Open for emergency access to Ogurki yard tracks

Rear side of mountain open for access to mainline tracks

Conventional open-grid construction to conserve height

L-girders

Heating duct

Backdrop merges into hill

Lally column

Eye level

CROSS SECTION B-B

Lift-the-flap scenery

Drop-leaf river

double track, the number of different combinations of meeting points between varying combinations of consists is infinite: A Class E6 4-4-2 hauling commuter coaches could meet an ore drag with helpers at Xovers one minute, an electric M.U. set from Chestnut Hole the next, and so on.

JAMMING IN THE GOODIES

To really exploit the potential of a railroad with several levels and with radius standards tailored to the equipment limitations for each different branch, we'll have to undertake some detailed design work of reasonable accuracy to make sure everything will fit. We'll also have to accept a few complications, such as the wild crossing on the main line near the turntable which makes the whole system of branch lines possible. Scenically it's not a bilevel plan, but the hidden trackage at Storch and Chestnut Hole is absolutely essential in terms of rolling-stock capacity and operating variety. The good news is that the three- and four-track rights of way can be built on sweeping, prototypical curves of generous radius—288 inches at some locations—without sacrificing a bit of space. We have to cheat a little here

and there: The third track between Llawn Mawr and Strathmore is actually the switching lead from Desmaigne Yard (if you can pronounce French names, the significance of that one will come to you, sooner or later), disguised with heavy ballasting to look like part of the main line. Likewise, the flying junction is not fully consummated but, rather, is merely suggested by the grading and direction of its four tracks as they disappear into three portals in true Pennsy style.

ELECTRIFICATION — AN EXTRA LITTLE CHALLENGE

Electrification of the commuter operation is left as an option, and the variety, quality, and availability of electric M.U. and locomotive kits or imports will probably have as much a part in the decision as anything else. The electrified trackage is arranged with practicality in mind. Wherever possible, electrified track is kept to the rear, reducing the likelihood that the catenary will be snagged by the forgetful railroader. And there's as little of it as necessary, just as in the prototype—expense in their case, plain hard work in ours.

The commuter line to Chestnut Hole could be operated solely with M.U.

The *Clocker* leaves North Philadelphia for a brief run ahead to 30th St and Broad St. Stations in downtown Philadelphia.

trains, so it could simply dead-end. Even if operated in steam or diesel, a runaround track could be sufficient; some Pennsy G5 Ten Wheelers had headlights and pilots on their tenders so that they could haul locals either-end-to.

WHAT'S IN A NAME?

Station and yard designations are deliberately phony, frenetic, or fanciful in keeping with the impracticality of modeling Pennsy prototypes without excessive selective compression. However, some of the Pennsylvania Dutch, Anglo-Saxon, Welsh, and industrial flavor found in names associated with the Berks/Bucks/Montgomery counties area of southeastern Pennsylvania is worked in amongst the bad puns. The serene stretch of river below Bee Falls recalls its canal-traffic days by retaining its name of Bee Haven (ports or harbors are sometimes referred to as havens). The real reason, of course, is to give the locals the chance each year to crown one of their young maidens as "Miss Bee Haven."

Ogurki Yard? That's "pickle" in Polish, and it recalls the shape of its trackage. If the real Pennsy can use Kase, Cork, View, and Cola as designations for its towers, we should have no restrictions on what we can do.

SIGNALS ARE A MUST

Certainly, signals are among the most attractive and fascinating parts of the railroad scene, and Pennsy's distinctive position-light signals are essential in characterizing this model for what it is.

From a bystander's point, they're interesting to watch, but the way you really get the feeling of being an integral part of the railroad is to run the trains by watching and interpreting the wayside signal aspects. This means walkaround control. The Schuylkill Division's aisleways are not totally convenient for following a mainline train without interruption because you have to backtrack around the center lobe when a train tunnels through the back of the layout. On the plus side, there are no duck-unders to negotiate unless you're working a local train at Johns Township.

Two-rail signaling is one of those frontiers that refuses to be crossed once and for all. There are literally dozens of workable circuits, but few of them are anywhere near ideal. If you want a complete system that accurately simulates the workings of its prototype in controlling bidirectional operations throughout a reasonably complicated layout, you've got yourself a project!

SCENERY – USING THE SAME SPACE TWICE

By now you've probably noticed that the only straight track on the entire main line (other than the short tangents between what would otherwise be intolerable S curves) is the section through Desmaigne Yard. Although there is very little covered trackage, the spaghetti-bowl effect has been minimized with only a single 20-foot section of double-faced backdrop, thanks to the layout's multi-lobe design.

The long curves through the Schuyl-kill Gorge climb toward Desmaigne Yard, which in contrast to yards on most layouts is at a high point of the main line. There isn't much choice in the matter because the space under the yard is desperately needed for storing trains, but the effect is good: The almost eye-level viewpoint makes for realistic switching operations and shows off the sides of the rolling stock rather than the roofs. Functioning derails may be necessary at the west ends of the yard tracks should the management elect to use any needle-axle rolling stock. A 0.5 per cent grade through the yard is necessary to keep the main line's eastward ruling grade at 1.4 per cent, and it is a figure not to be exceeded if cars are to stay put for reliable automatic-coupler switching.

Like all good track plans with passenger stations of reasonable busyness, the Schuylkill Division boasts one double-slip switch—enough to show off your prowess without the rapidly diminishing level of fun that comes with installing the second and succeeding double-slip switches! Unfortunately, although the location of the Lally column provides the space problem that justifies the double slip, it also forces the switch to the rear of the yard where its intricacies aren't as visible as we'd like.

We'll have to depend on the yardmaster to keep things moving enough to let the double-slip be seen and appreciated periodically.

A Mushroom in the Bedroom

Innovative multi-deck design squeezes a "lifetime"

Sn3 layout into a 12 x 14-foot room

WHAT'S THE nicest place to build a model railroad? Not the common basement, garage, or attic! The bedroom or other civilized "spare" room is it. With a high, finished ceiling that won't shed dirt, a generally temperate climate summer or winter, a room door that keeps the contents secure, and a minimum of such layout-height obstacles as ducts or drain pipes, it's simply more comfortable as a site for your empire building. Even the floor is easier on your arches.

Assuming the family situation is such that the "lease" on this idyllic space won't be revoked in the foreseeable future, what's the rub? Space. The typical bedroom is on the small side for a "lifetime" layout, one that will provide detailing and operating challenges and opportunities over a substantial model railroading career. Also, in houses built within the past 80 years or so, there's almost always a closet as far as possible from the entrance door. Naturally, crawl-under access to this closet isn't acceptable.

SPACE UTILIZATION: 125 PERCENT

In mitigating these difficulties, the plan for the Western Colorado Ry. fits 196 square feet of top-level, "scenick-able" model railroad into a room with a total floor area of 158 square feet (12 x 12 plus a 2 x 7-foot entryway) while maintaining a 24"-wide aisleway to a closet in the far corner and walkaround access to all mainline points.

The key, of course, is double-decking. With that 8-foot ceiling there's height aplenty for two decks, maintaining good headroom above the top layer and the 15" to 20" separation between levels desirable for independent appreciation of the separate scenes. That's nice, but how can you look at the trains from a desirable eye level on both decks? The answer is a raised floor beside the upper deck—not just a short step up, but a full 21" to match the vertical separation of the two realms. Now, if only a single deck could be seen from any one point . . . .

That's where the "mushroom" comes in. As shown in the cross-section of fig.

1, the raised platform in the fat "stem" of the mushroom opens up vistas over an irregular doughnut of upper-level railroad extending over the track, scenery, and aisles below. These expansive views are inside an irregular loop of backdrop—freestanding, an up-turned rim on the mushroom cap, if you will—blocking any awareness of something extraneous below.

Down below is a conventional walk-in layout equally isolated from the sights and goings-on topside—the

---

Author's Insight

No doubt about it—building and detailing the Western Colorado can absorb more man-hours per square foot of floor space than any other plan in this book. Although the trackwork required in this Sn3 plan is commercially available, in exchange for the relative comfort of working in a bedroom there is the challenge of engineering a complex structure that goes far beyond the sophistication of what we think of as conventional "bench-work." Getting some of the chunks of railroad into place may involve planning of almost ship-model-in-a-bottle cleverness.

In return, a ridiculous amount of railroading is crammed into a 12 x 14-foot room, and stand-up access to the closet is

maintained. With a reasonable amount of hidden trackage, viewing of all segments of the line is at a comfortable, no-scroonch eye level, with only one level visible at all points. The secret, of course, is the "mushroom" configuration, in combination with selection of a prototype that penetrates largely vertical terrain with sharp curves and steep grades.

Getting from one level to the other takes an (ugh!) helix. The very same helix serves in up and down directions and, double-track with curved crossovers, provides multi-train midrun staging, squeezing benefits from the hidden trackage it entails.

"ground" around the mushroom stem. With the upper-deck structure just above head height and the lower-level at near-optimum viewing and comfort elevations (we can only say "near" because the optimum height depends on the eye level of the proprietor and remains a matter of opinion), the mushroom averts the usual double-deck irritations of "scroonching" down for a look at the lower-deck scene and knocking your head on the upper deck upon straightening up.

But how does the railroad get from down below to up above? With a helix, of course, though that's not without drawbacks. Minimizing them is a subject we can take up later; now we need to know more about the Western Colorado.

LAID OUT FOR MODELING

Like the Western Maryland, Clinchfield, and Colorado Midland, the Western Colorado was surveyed and built with the model railroader in mind. Traversing largely vertical terrain, its steep grades, sharp curves, and heavy mineral traffic called for the use of a lot of powerful but compact locomotives to pull and shove fairly short trains amid almost fanciful scenery.

The determined Scottish entrepreneur who threaded the WC through some of the Western Slope's most inaccessible territory during the narrow gauge boom of the late 1800s also did the modeler the favor of picking a locale that would remain virtually highwayless for decades. When the authorities did finally find a way to build a road to the WC's far terminus in the 1930s, its route was circuitous. So roundabout, in fact, that a 3-foot gauge passenger schedule based on 22-mph average speeds was still competitive enough to keep the Western Colorado's short varnish consists connecting fairly profitably with the fabled Denver & Rio Grande Western San Juan well into the late 1940s—which happens to be the period of our replica.

The junction with the Rio Grande's longest-lived narrow gauge route was

In a setting that could inspire the West Park scene on the Sn3 Western Colorado Railway, the *San Juan* climbs the west slope of Cumbres Pass in 1948.

in such a confined canyon that the WC had no choice but Skye for locating its engine terminal, main yard, and headquarters. Skye may seem an unlikely "division point" because it's near the summit of the main line, but so was Bluefield, West Virginia, on the Norfolk & Western, come to think of it. And as the most populous point in this wide-open country, Skye boasts the line's largest passenger and express station.

Like the fabled Uintah Railway a couple of hundred miles to the northwest, the WC connected two points at about the same elevation, but in different watersheds separated by a horrendous mountain ridge. The far end of the WC is at Oban—there being no previous communities worthy of names, the railroad's builder took the liberty of tagging points on the line with appellations borrowed from Scotland.

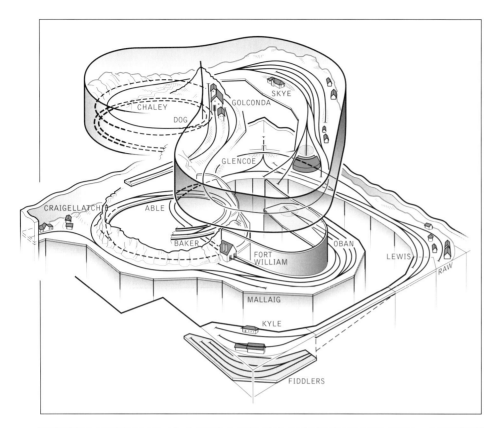

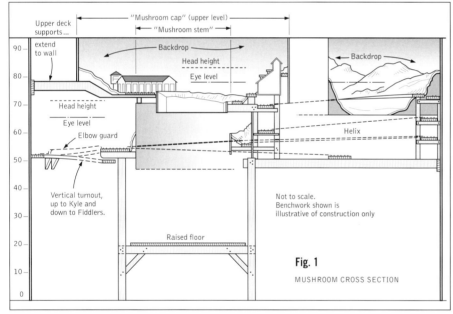

Fig. 1

MUSHROOM CROSS SECTION

profile of the Western Colorado, several approaches can be combined to reduce the magnitude of Project Helix and to make every inch of space and foot of track give its all:

• One helix takes the main up one side of the mountain and down the other.

• The lowest and highest turns of the helix are mostly open and scenicked.

• Trains get off to a flying start in both directions, gaining considerable elevation before entering the corkscrew. With the 4 percent grade appropriate for this line, just two turns out of sight provide the 15" of additional rise necessary for comfortable separation between the decks. Given the 30" minimum radius the mushroom allows, this interturn spacing is a very comfortable 7½ ".
(Incidentally, the steeper the grade on any helix, the better from the standpoint of access for maintenance and rerailing.)

• The helix is double-tracked, not to carry dense traffic but to let it serve as a layover / staging track resource that represents half or so of the whole railroad's capacity for absorbing rolling stock. Properly parked behind a crossover, 3 trains with a total of 30 of those stubby freight cars can be in various out-of-sight stages of progress along the route without blocking mainline traffic in either direction. Trains may have to follow a wiggly route through alternating facing and trailing-point crossovers, but they can get through.

In terms of space, double-tracking the helix is a bargain. For typical radii and track centers, the extra width is less than 10 percent. And curved crossovers with minimum radius on the inside legs of the turnouts can make the helix a dispatching asset in only 20 percent more space than a single-track spiral.

RIDING THE LINE

To appreciate the extent to which this prosperous little road maintains Class I pretensions, let's take a trip on the "Limited," a twice-a-week schedule primarily justified by traffic from the mountain resort at Oban and the only first-class run on the timetable.

(Daily passenger service is provided by mixed trains. Their second-class timetable status still makes them superior to the third-class and extra freights that haul most of the ore and timber, and the WC runs the mixeds closely enough to schedule to serve the significant local passenger, express, mail, and package-freight traffic.)

A well-maintained C-16 2-8-0 hauls

Coal mined around Oban was of such low quality that it wasn't worth a trip over the line to outside consumers. However, it did make nearby Fort William a logical place for a coal-fueled smelter to convert ore from the Castle Drum Mine at Glencoe into a refined product well worth the trip back to the Rio Grande connection at Kyle.

DE-HORNING THE HELIX

Now, what about minimizing those unsavory characteristics of the helix

connecting the lowland ends of our point-to-point main line with the alpine crossing of the mountain range? A helix takes considerable space: Its diameter must be 2+ times the minimum radius. A good part of every train's journey, at best shorter than you'd like, is out of sight and therefore uninteresting. Construction, though not as challenging as scratchbuilding a double-slip switch in Z scale, is something you'd enjoy more in retrospect than in the process.

As shown in the schematic and

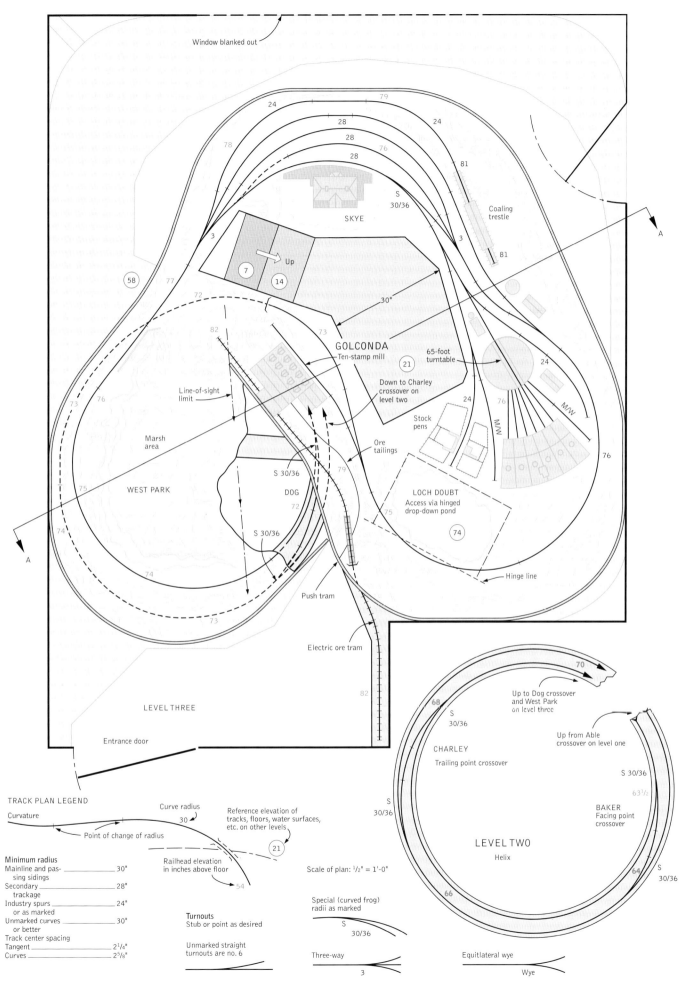

Window blanked out

24
79
28
24
78
28
76
28
S
30/36
81
Coaling
trestle
SKYE
81
3
3
58
77
7   Up
14
30"
72
82
GOLCONDA
Ten-stamp mill
65-foot
turntable
24
73
Line-of-sight
limit
21
76
M/W
73
76
Down to Charley
crossover on
level two
Stock
pens
24
76
M/W
Marsh
area
76
Ore tailings
79
S 30/36
WEST PARK
75
DOG
72
LOCH DOUBT
Access via hinged
drop-down pond
74
75
S 30/36
74
74
Hinge line
73
Push tram
Electric ore tram
82
LEVEL THREE
Entrance door

70

Up to Dog crossover
and West Park
on level three
68
S
30/36
CHARLEY
Up from Able
crossover on level one
Trailing point crossover
S 30/36
S
30/36
63½
BAKER
Facing point
crossover
LEVEL TWO
Helix
64
S
30/36
66

TRACK PLAN LEGEND
Curvature

Curve radius
30
Reference elevation of
tracks, floors, water surfaces,
etc. on other levels
21

Point of change of radius

Minimum radius
Mainline and pas-   30"
  sing sidings
Secondary   28"
  trackage
Industry spurs   24"
  or as marked
Unmarked curves   30"
  or better
Track center spacing
Tangent   2¼"
Curves   2⅝"

Railhead elevation
in inches above floor
54

Scale of plan: ½" = 1'-0"

Special (curved frog)
radii as marked
S
30/36

Turnouts
Stub or point as desired

Unmarked straight
turnouts are no. 6

Three-way
3

Equitlateral wye

Wye

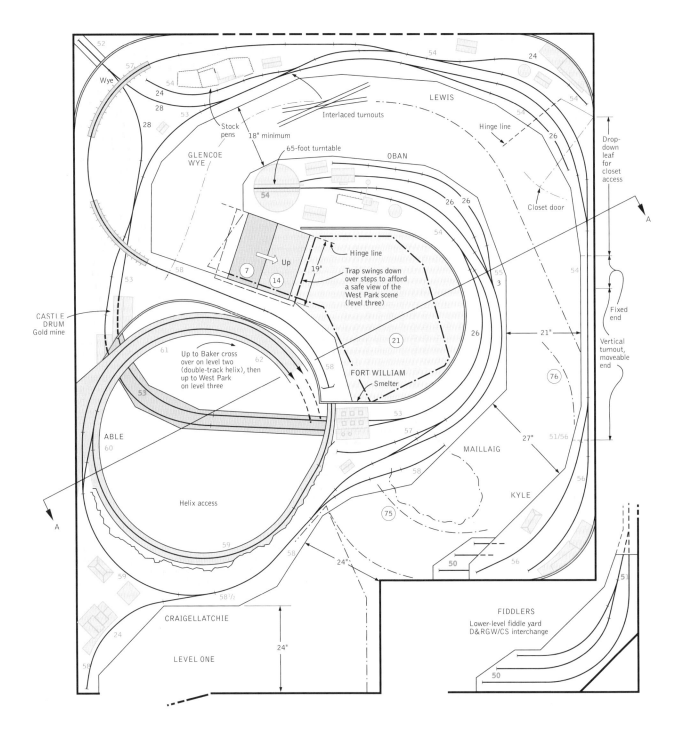

52

57

Wye

24

28

28

53

GLENCOE
WYE

Stock
pens

18" minimum

Interlaced turnouts

65-foot turntable

54

54

54

LEWIS

Hinge line

54

24

26

54

Drop-
down
leaf
for
closet
access

OBAN

26   26

54

Closet door

A

CASTLE
DRUM
Gold mine

53

58

61

62

Up to Baker cross
over on level two
(double-track helix), then
up to West Park
on level three

53

ABLE

60

Helix access

A

59

59

59

58½

CRAIGELLATCHIE

58

LEVEL ONE

7   14

Up

19"

Hinge line

Trap swings down
over steps to afford
a safe view of the
West Park scene
(level three)

21

FORT WILLIAM
Smelter

58

53

57

58

75

24"

55
3

26

21"

76

27"   51/56

MAILLAIG

KYLE

56

51

50

56

50

24"

Fixed
end

Vertical
turnout,
moveable
end

FIDDLERS
Lower-level fiddle yard
D&RGW/CS interchange

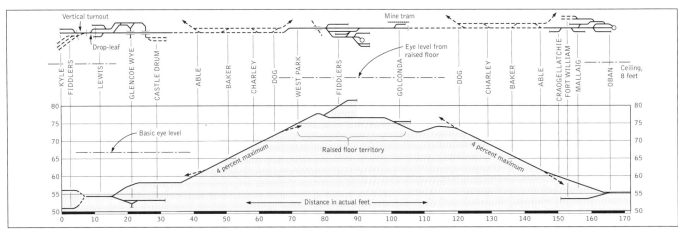

Vertical turnout

Drop-leaf

Mine tram

Eye level from
raised floor

Ceiling,
8 feet

KYLE
FIDDLERS
LEWIS
GLENCOE WYE
CASTLE DRUM
ABLE
BAKER
CHARLEY
DOG
WEST PARK
FIDDLERS
GOLCONDA
DOG
CHARLEY
BAKER
ABLE
CRAIGELLATCHIE
FORT WILLIAM
MAILLAIG
OBAN

80

75

70

65

60

55

50

Basic eye level

4 percent maximum

Raised floor territory

4 percent maximum

Distance in actual feet

80

75

70

65

60

55

50

0   10   20   30   40   50   60   70   80   90   100   110   120   130   140   150   160   170

the Limited's three cars at speeds as smart as its saucer-sized drivers and the curvature of the equally well-maintained track will permit. Like most of the Western Colorado's mainline motive power, the Consolidation is a Rio Grande hand-me-down.

Readying the train for departure was complicated by the fact that at Oban only the last couple of car-lengths of yard track and the turntable itself—the only runaround connection—are level. Everything else, including the tracks coming up from the Fort William smelter, tilts up or down at 2 percent or worse.

By the time our Limited passes the spurs at Mallaig, the grade has stiffened to the 4 percent that's standard for the WC in both directions. The passenger train, of course, needs no helper. Add a car, though, and one of the K-28 Mikados would have to be assigned.

The ascending train remains in the open though in the shadow of near-vertical cliffs as it passes another spur at Craigellatchie and disappears around the bend. Like other Colorado narrow gauge lines of its era, the WC squeezes its way through the mountains with a minimum of tunneling. Our miniature version manages to sneak in and out of the hidden helix four times with only one exposed tunnel portal.

Inside the helix, the Limited passes the morning mixed (which left Oban an hour earlier) and meets a train of ore from Castle Drum bound for Fort William via Oban. Out in the sunshine again but still climbing, our little train enters West Park country—one of those surprisingly level spots amid the Rockies like its counterpart Estes, Middle, and South Parks east of the Divide.

West Park is beautiful, with a meandering stream below the curving track and the majestic mountain range in the distance looking almost like a painted backdrop. It's a pity the terrain is such that pioneering railfans (remember, this is the late 1940s) found that only distant photos of the trains were practical. Rather than slog across the intervening marshland, the smart ones learned to appreciate an occasional view emphasizing the tininess of the whole train dwarfed by the mountain majesties.

A LOFTY HUB

Finally cresting the summit after one last stream crossing, the Limited makes its only intermediate stop at the metropolis of this lofty, remote country, Skye. The passenger station there is made

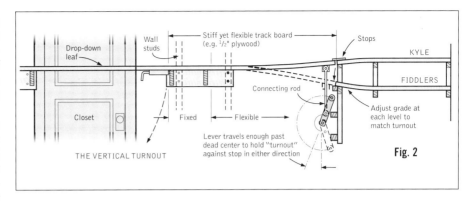

THE VERTICAL TURNOUT

Fig. 2

more imposing by the WC corporate offices upstairs. As the operating hub of the line, it features the railroad's only locomotive coaling trestle and a six-stall enginehouse with turntable. Two turntables would ordinarily be one too many for a model railroader to maintain, but of course these are manually operated—no problem.

Skye's sprawling sidings mostly hold an assortment of that irresistible narrow gauge maintenance-of-way equipment: a rotary plow, a pile driver, and a derrick, each with its own tender, water car, or idler flat. During the stock season, when cattle and sheep that summered in the surrounding high pastures are shipped to lower altitudes, the railroad must find other roosts for its non-revenue equipment to free tracks serving the pens.

Yard tracks elsewhere in Skye are adequate, but just barely. Only one through track is of full mainline radius, so care is in order when a Mikado must venture toward one of the sharper curves. A reminder of the WC's early days is the prevalence here of stub turnouts, three-way and others. Point switches have replaced stubs at other places along the line, but Skye's heavy snowfall is a good argument for keeping the rail-benders: They make snow sweeping a lot easier. Just don't try throwing a stub switch while a pony truck is resting on it. . . .

DOWN – NOT QUITE THE SAME WAY

Already starting downward, the Limited circles picturesque Loch Doubt and sweeps past the most impressive structure in the area, the ten-stamp mill at Golconda, processing ore from a hardrock mine. Far up the hillside is an electric tram that brings raw ore from the diggings to the top story of the mill, and then gravity moves it through the pulverizing and concentration process. A 2-foot gauge push tram suffices to explain how the mine tailings are

dumped, out of sight and mind, behind the backdrop. Mine concentrate moves out in boxcars over the WC.

Ducking into a tunnel portal just a bit taller than you might expect—that pile driver rides almost 17 feet above the rail even folded and locked down—Lewis-bound trains re-enter the same helix they ascended en route to Skye. Our Limited passes a train of empties bound for Glencoe and Castle Drum between "Charley" and "Baker," and crosses over at the latter point to emerge from the helix beyond "Able" on the right track (the left one, in this case) to bring us into Lewis. The dispatcher has to think ahead on this railroad: A misrouting at "Baker" would send the train back to its origin at Oban.

The rest of the trip to Lewis is also scenic. Two trestles take us over the Castle Drum Mine tracks and the Glencoe wye tail, and alongside a canyon. With no tracks hiding below, that gorge can be a deep one!

Most of our passengers are headed for the Rio Grande connection, so the Limited chuffs right into a stub track at Kyle. As soon as its connecting passengers have unloaded, the little train backs up to Lewis, where any of the locals may detrain. The C-16 backs around its train, turns on the Glencoe wye, and is ready for the return trip.

There's no surplus of track at Lewis either, so the morning mixed that follows the Limited into this terminal would have no place to disassemble itself if the Limited didn't immediately back to Kyle and park in the second stub track. Mixed-train patrons have plenty of time to get off at Lewis while the crew distributes its boxcars here and there, finally pushing the coach and baggage-mail car to Kyle.

WHAT'S A "VERTICAL TURNOUT"?

With relatively heavy on-line freight traffic such as the livestock and Castle Drum-Fort William ore movements, the

Western Colorado isn't entirely dependent on the Rio Grande interchange. As a result of bad blood between the lines in the past, the interchange isn't at Lewis or Kyle, but an out-of-the-way set of spurs called Fiddlers. The many reefers, boxcars, and tank cars stored here could in no other way be accommodated by the WC's visible tracks.

Connecting this den of mild iniquity to the main track at Lewis is a "vertical turnout"—simply a 48" plank (fig. 2) firmly attached to the wall at the left end and flexible enough to bend up 2" or down 3" to connect with either of two stacked levels, The generous vertical spacing, twice the height of the tallest Sn3 rolling stock, allows hand room for fiddling freight cars on the lower deck. There we can reconcile the size of the car roster with the capacity of the railroad and, incidentally, convey the idea that the WC interchanged with the Colorado & Southern (during its existence) as well as with the Rio Grande.

IT DOESN'T HAVE TO BE SN3

With no change to the track plan, the Western Colorado can be built as an Sn3½ railroad to make use of HO standard gauge track, wheelsets, locomotive mechanisms, and the like, with superstructures and roadbed in ³⁄₁₆" scale, 1:64 proportion. That would be most appropriate for modeling the wilder parts of the 3½-foot gauge railways found all over the world, from Newfoundland and Japan to Australia and South Africa.

What about an HO standard gauge version representing a similarly rugged route? After all, the Colorado Midland was standard gauge, just as steep, and but for the World War I demand for scrap iron, might have hung on into the more popular late-steam modeling era. Since HO standard gauge rolling stock is generally a little narrower and considerably (½" or so) lower in height than ³⁄₁₆" scale Sn3 or Sn3½ equipment, there's no question about its compatibility with the clearances and track centers of this plan as is.

Four percent grades are perhaps on the steep side for your more commonplace mountain short line. A simple modification that keeps the mushroom's comfortable spacing between decks is to add one turn to the helix. Readjusting the grades approaching and through the helix results in a uniform 2.8 percent slope. The 30" radius is luxurious in the smaller scale, and the turn-to-turn vertical separation in the helix at 2.8 percent is almost 5½"—with reasonably shallow roadbed construction, enough to leave the essential handwidth access between layers.

What about those crossovers that make the helix so useful? If this "stretch limo" helix has the same number and alternating trailing-point/facing-point sequence of crossovers but their spacing is revised, it will have the same three "sidings" or parking places. However, two of them will be of double length, thus accommodating the longer trains that those lighter grades will encourage. Since a typical 30-foot Sn3 boxcar is almost exactly the same length as a 40-foot standard gauge HO car, assembling longer trains in the yards at Oban and Lewis will test the ingenuity of the train crews.

S scalers of necessity are generally not fazed by the prospect of building or commissioning those curved turnouts that make the versatile double-track helix fit the space available—straight-frog no. 5 crossovers would add 16" to its long axis. HO scale aficionados who want to take advantage of all the products available will realize that coming down to a 24" minimum radius that's very reasonable for this period short line will allow use of straight-frog no. 5s within the same length.

Curved turnouts are available in HO with no. 7 frogs and 24" and 28" radii, and they'll do the job in about 10" less. Those inches can be put toward any number of good purposes, including fitting the plan into an 11-foot room or relaxing the slopes of the often blatantly vertical scenery.

STONE-AGE CONTROL

With or without some form of command control to match each cab with its train, how do you determine that a train has reached a "parking place" inside the helix when it's been out of sight for half a scale mile or more? No doubt this could be done with an elaborate system of optical sensors or detection circuits. There's a simpler way, however, if you're not allergic to caveman technology at this late date.

All it takes is a set of stopping sections at the strategic locations turned off by turnout position or (gasp!) toggle switch. Approach at something less than warp speed, and when the train stops you know where it is. You do, of course, have to know that the train is shorter than the passing track. Without reference markers along the right of way approaching the secluded tracks, a computer program comparing the sum of the coupled lengths of each car and locomotive in the consist with the distance between clearance points can do the same thing far more elegantly—assuming no errors in typing the engine and car numbers!